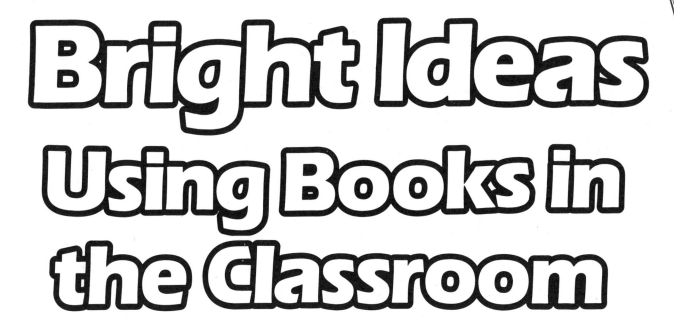

Bright Ideas
Using Books in the Classroom

Written by Hazel Short

Contents

Published by Scholastic Publications Ltd,
Marlborough House, Holly Walk,
Leamington Spa, Warwickshire CV32 4LS.

Written by Hazel Short
Edited by Christine Lee
Sub-edited by Jane Morgan
Illustrations by Helen Herbert

Printed in Great Britain by
Loxley Brothers Ltd, Sheffield

ISBN 0 590 76015 7

Front and back cover: designed by Sue Limb,
Photographs by Martyn Chilmaid.

Introduction

The title of this book refers to the use of books for literature-based projects. This is not a new idea and in many nursery and infant classrooms there are fine examples of books which have been brought to life by display, model-making and acting. Sometimes, however, these ideas can be extended further and used most successfully throughout the whole primary range.

There are no written rules governing literature-based projects. They simply provide another vehicle for teaching good language skills, using books for information, practical mathematics, science activities and indeed can be extended to all areas of the curriculum.

While becoming increasingly interested in what motivates children to learn to read and enjoy books, I have realised that these projects need not be confined to fiction, but with the wealth of non-fiction material and poetry available in schools, exciting work can be done in these areas also. With the research now being done on learning to read, I have come to understand the valuable contribution that this area of teaching makes.

AIMS AND OBJECTIVES

Your aim might simply be to promote good literature and the love of books which is a worthy aim in itself. A supply of good books in the classroom and throughout the school, the availability of book clubs or bookshops, visiting authors and librarians, and the teacher's own enthusiasm, will all help in realising this aim. It may be that you wish to use this approach as a means of teaching higher order reading and language skills, such as cloze procedure, word deletion, sequencing, different styles of writing or discussion.

Links made with fact rather than fiction can also be used to teach children how to use books for information. This could include how to use the library, alphabetical order, index and contents pages and how to use a dictionary.

You may also wish to try and develop the book and its story and make connections with other areas of the curriculum.

ORGANISATION

Work can be done by individual members of the class, by groups, or by a mixture of both; the project may be just for one class, or produced for other classes to share and read. Juniors always enjoy sharing their work and writing stories for infants. The work, therefore, needs to be visual and as characters, scenes and written work develop, it should be displayed and given as much room as possible.

The length of time which is devoted to a project is entirely up to the teacher. It may be that a book has been chosen to complement a topic already started. Alternatively, it may be that the book has not been chosen because of any links or follow-up work, in which case a lesser proportion of time may be devoted to it. Or it could be the main influence on your work in the classroom at one particular time. My most successful topics have been done in this way, and you might find that as your enthusiasm takes off, so your project extends, not leaving any time for any other topic work.

I have found no better way of introducing myself to a class in September than by using a literature-based project. Because of all the different ways you have to work while doing this, the class soon understands your methods of organisation. The children become confident and are soon able to settle down and work well in a group situation.

DEVELOPMENT OF LANGUAGE

Here is a wonderful opportunity to develop and extend language skills in all areas: speech, reading and writing.

Of all the areas, writing can be extended more than any other. Not all children are naturally creative, yet at school we expect them to write constantly, perhaps more than at any other time of their lives. I believe that writing can be taught and developed. In literature-based projects there are many opportunities to teach different writing styles, as will be seen in the examples in this book, but creative writing is perhaps the most difficult. A careful choice of books, however, will give the children good examples to follow. If an apprenticeship approach can be used to teach reading then a similar way can be found to teach writing. As you read your chosen book, look carefully for examples of writing at its best. I call this looking at writer's tricks.

Look at alliteration, onomatopoeia and metaphors; you need not label them as such, but encourage their use in prose and poetry. Children of all ages, infant and junior, will respond to this in some way. One of my children once wrote 'the branches of the tree were like the crooked fingers of an old witch' – a far more exciting description than just saying 'the tree had bent branches'.

CURRICULUM

There are no limits to how you can make successful curriculum links. As you read a book, ideas will spring to mind, perhaps not at the first reading, but at the second and the third. They should not be forced, but if ideas occur to help bring a story to life or develop work in a particular area then the opportunity should be taken. Books often have an historic or geographical flavour and this nearly always provides a way of producing some maths work such as comparison, graphs, estimating or time. Sometimes science experiments help to bring certain chapters to life, and there are

CRRRAAAASSSSSSH!
CRASH!
CRASH!
CRASH!

always opportunities for incorporating drama. There is no better way of following a story and its characters than to develop the role of these characters dramatically.

Similarly music projects are often in evidence and endless opportunities for art and craft such as paintings, drawings, three-dimensional work, fabric and thread work all emerge as the story unfolds. All that is required is a lively mind, both on the teacher's part and on that of the children. Children sometimes come up with brilliant ideas, which you may never have thought of, but which need to be pursued. After all, this is all part of the aim of using literature-based projects.

APPROACHES

Find a book that you really like. If you are in any doubt discard the title as this may lead to failure before very long. Assess your children. As all teachers know, a book which is loved by one class might not be enjoyed by another. If therefore you decide to begin a new school year with a literature-based topic, you need to choose an all-time favourite which you know will succeed.

Read the book carefully. Read it again and again. Each time you have an idea, jot it down otherwise you might forget it. Obvious ideas for work will spring to mind at the first reading, but as you read it again ideas may emerge from small phrases and sentences, particularly in the area of language skills.

Don't close your mind to further ideas; make a plan or a flow chart but leave room for further expansion at a later date. Don't feel that you have to tackle all areas; be prepared to discard some as you go along just as you would in tackling any other area of the curriculum.

Decide where your starting point is going to be. It may not necessarily be at the

beginning of the book. For example, in tackling *The Hobbit*, I began by reading the description of Smaug, who makes his appearance towards the end of the book. We started by making an enormous dragon, so big that every member of the class had a hand in its construction. This instantly motivated the class and they were eager to hear the whole story.

Decide whether you are going to read the entire book or just part of it. Is it going to be your main topic work or an offshoot of another topic you intend to tackle? Plan your display areas and start collecting together any material you might need. Decide whether your work lends itself to mobiles or hanging displays from the ceiling as these add greatly to the

atmosphere by bringing an exciting mood to the topic.

Are you going to involve any other classes? For what audience is this work intended? Will they have a chance to see your class's work?

If you are required to give a class assembly once a term as is the case in many primary schools, this could be a good way of showing other children what you have been doing. It promotes enthusiasm for literature and also makes other children eager to read the book; it may, therefore, be useful to have more than one copy so that children can borrow them. I find that you can always link books with assembly themes, be they religious or social. Thanks

can be given for the gift of sight, the ability to be able to learn to read, for books and authors, etc.

You may decide not to read the ending of the book so that the children can make up their own endings. You can then supply the real ending or leave it up to them to find out. You might on the other hand read the ending and ask them to write a small sequel, a 'what happened next'.

Any work not on display might be kept by the children in individual folders or books, or you might produce one or two class books depending on the amount of work you have. Include illustrations. These always provide a good opportunity to look at the layout of books. The children can then work

on contents pages, indexes, numbering of pages, lists of illustrations and, with older children, bibliographies. Even with younger children I ask them to supply authors and titles of books they have used for information.

You will soon know if your choice of book has been successful. When you come to the point where you have to say 'we will have to leave it there for today' there should be a chorus of groans. The topic should generate constant chatter and usually children will present you with extra work they have done at home, such as little drawings, stories or models.

Hazel Short

8

CHARTING WORK

Literature-based projects need not be complicated, simple charts will show the versatility and the range of topics which such projects can encompass. The following three examples show the composition of typical literature-based projects.

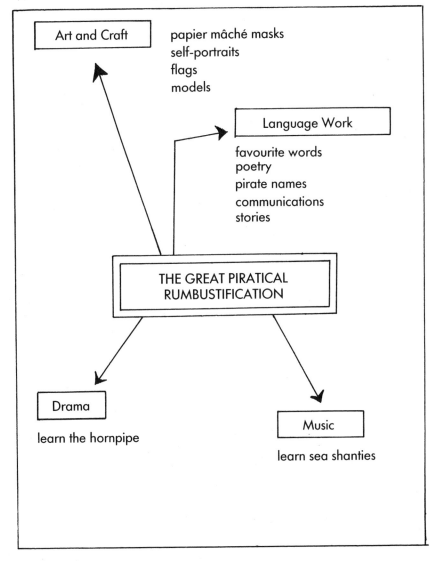

Art and Craft
- papier mâché masks
- self-portraits
- flags
- models

Language Work
- favourite words
- poetry
- pirate names
- communications
- stories

THE GREAT PIRATICAL RUMBUSTIFICATION

Drama
- learn the hornpipe

Music
- learn sea shanties

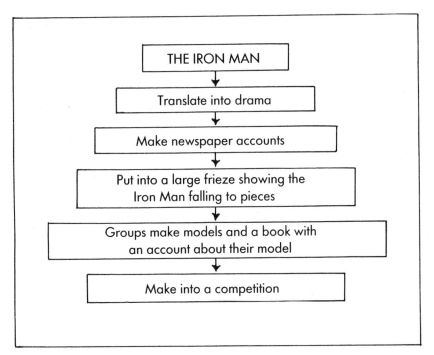

THE IRON MAN
↓
Translate into drama
↓
Make newspaper accounts
↓
Put into a large frieze showing the Iron Man falling to pieces
↓
Groups make models and a book with an account about their model
↓
Make into a competition

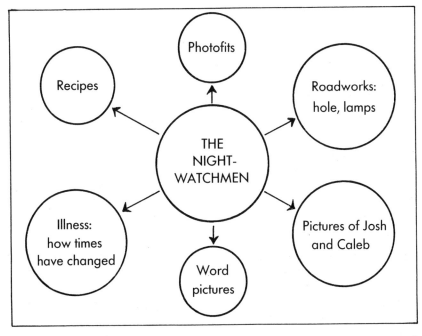

THE NIGHT-WATCHMEN
- Photofits
- Recipes
- Roadworks: hole, lamps
- Pictures of Josh and Caleb
- Word pictures
- Illness: how times have changed

Fiction books

The use of fiction is, perhaps, the most obvious choice for a literature-based project, being the area of literature that children are most familiar with.

The following books are all tried and tested classroom favourites and range in style from fantasy, as in *The Hobbit*, to humour, as in *The Great Piratical Rumbustification*. Apart from written work and art and craft work, the books give an opportunity for numerous related topics such as geography (*The Wheel on the School*), the study of plant life (*The Bongleweed*) or the study of animals (*The Siege of White Deer Park*). All the activities can be adapted to suit age requirements or limitations imposed by the size and layout of the classroom.

The Iron Man
Ted Hughes (Faber)

'His eyes, like headlamps, glowed white, then red, then infra-red, searching the sea.'

Age range
Seven to eleven.

Synopsis
The story reads almost like poetry, which is not surprising as its author is the Poet Laureate. From the first word, the children are instantly gripped by the story which follows. The Iron Man is a huge monster. He has an enormous appetite, feeding on metal only, which ranges from tractors to motor cars. But with the help of Hogarth, a little boy, he is able to find another source of food, thus alleviating the distress that he has caused the community. More importantly, he helps to save the world from destruction and becomes the world's hero.

Setting the scene
Surprise the children. Cover display boards with black backing paper. In large letters, in white chalk, either write out the first paragraph of the book or write

'and the Iron Man stepped forward, off the cliff, into nothingness.
CRRRAAAASSSSSSSH! . . .
CRASH!
CRASH!
CRASH!'

Add some yellow stars around the caption. This should promote some discussion when the children come into the room. Leave a corner large enough for displaying models.

Musical drama

Age range
Seven to nine.

Group size
Whole class or groups.

What you need
Space for drama, musical instruments.

What to do
Read the first chapter to the class. Then go back and, breaking the chapter down into smaller sections, read through it again, so that the children have the chance to dwell on every word. Eight and nine-year-olds enjoy learning the first two pages off by heart, with different children contributing to different sections. Words can be discussed and each piece of the Iron Man's anatomy can be visualised, thinking about his size and the comparisons to be made with everyday objects.

A good way of exploring this further is through drama. By linking arms and legs together, groups of children can become the Iron Man's head, arms and legs. There are always children who love to act the role played by his eyes. Warm-up sessions can include the fall of the Iron Man, with musical instruments used to represent the sound of the 'CRRRAAAASSSSSSSH!' Children can experiment here and decide which instruments will produce the best effect. This will produce such questions as 'Will the sound build up from quiet to loud', or 'Will it grow quieter and peter out gradually?' The fun begins when the children work at putting the Iron Man back together again. How are the children going to act out being the hand? What will they do when they meet up with the eye? There is work here for several sessions but it is important that the words in the book are followed closely, because this is the magic and the very essence of *The Iron Man*.

Newspaper reports

Age range
Eight to eleven.

Group size
Individuals.

What you need
A collection of newspapers with as many different typefaces as possible, jotters, paper for written work, scissors, pencils, pens, crayons, black sugar paper, adhesive.

CRRRAAAASSSSSSH!

Mystery metal found on beach

Iron wreckage shocks townspeople

Iron Man's body found
— police baffled

Falling metal horror
Eye-witness account

What to do
Encourage the children to search through newspapers for suitable headlines, or parts of headlines which can be carefully cut out. Encourage them to look through magazines at home.

Ask the children to write a report of the Iron Man's fall as though they were there on the cliff. They must write the report as if they were a newspaper reporter. Ask them to do suitable illustrations. Don't show them a drawing of the Iron Man, but see if the details they have learnt about him come out in their illustrations.

Display the work either by pasting up headlines across a display board and putting individual work underneath, or use large sheets of sugar paper and ask the children to produce writing in columns, so that it can be cut out and put with individual headlines as in a newspaper. Give the newspaper a title.

Daily Blah

Iron Man falls from cliff

Pictures in words

Age range
Seven to eleven.

Group size
Individuals.

What you need
Paper, pencils, pens, crayons.

What to do
This activity can be done instead of or in addition to the newspaper report. Ask the children to create a word picture of the Iron Man's fall. Explain that 'word pictures' are a way of 'painting a picture in words' – this is a good means of introducing poetry to them. Tell them that in a word picture every word counts; if it's not necessary then don't use it. This also helps to overcome the difficulties of using rhyme. Give them lots of examples.

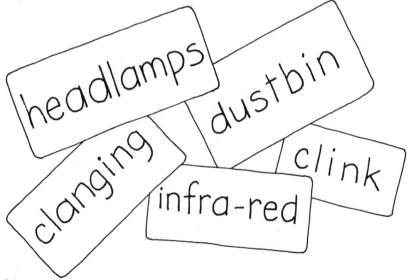

Because of the structure of the first chapter, by just altering and adding a few words even children with writing difficulties can achieve a successful, satisfying piece of work. These can be illustrated and displayed on walls or made into a class book, which will become a useful addition to the book corner. For younger children you might like to put useful words on cards. By juggling these around and adding their own words, they can create their own poems.

Making a frieze

Age range
Seven to eleven.

Group size
Small groups.

What you need
Large sheets of white paper suitable for painting, paints, a variety of brushes, foil. Optional: junk material including cardboard boxes and tubes; papier mâché, stapler, adhesive, sticky tape.

What to do
Divide the class into groups and ask the children to draw and paint the various parts of the Iron Man's body as it falls to pieces. To help keep the body in proportion, give each group paper of an appropriate size and explain that they must use the whole sheet. The groups will have to co-operate so that the legs, arms, hands and eyes look as though they belong to the same creature. Mark in the top, bottom and sides of the figure to be drawn to give the children a guide-line. Cut the pieces out, leaving a thin border of white around each one so that they will stand out when displayed. Discuss with the children what colour of paint should be used.

As an alternative to using paint, a striking effect can be obtained by making a collage with suitable metallic paper or cooking foil. When the pieces have been cut out, arrange them on your original black backing paper with the words and stars as though they were falling through the air.

You might instead like to build a model out of cardboard. Junk material, including large cardboard boxes and tubes for legs can be stuck or stapled together. The eyes are an important feature, so build these up from papier mâché then paint them to express their changing colours.

Do not over-instruct the children – they will use reels of sticky tape if they are left unchecked, but there will always be somebody in the group with really bright ideas, whatever their age. If the children can make a model with moving parts, all the better.

Making a monster

Age range
Nine to eleven.

Group size
Groups of up to six.

What you need
Junk material such as boxes, yoghurt pots, cardboard tubes, card and string; paint, adhesive, paper and binding for making class books.

What to do
Divide the class into groups and ask each group to invent their own monster, name it and build it out of the junk material available, making sure that it will stand or sit properly. Then ask each group to make a story as Ted Hughes did with the Iron Man. Each person in the group should write a chapter and illustrate it suitably. Stress that someone should write a good beginning, someone an ending, and others the middle parts. The book will need a cover, a contents page, a list of illustrations, and the pages should be numbered. Give

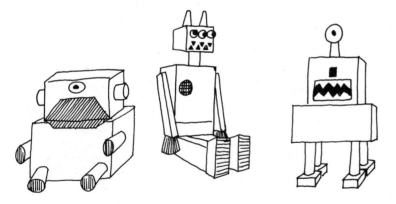

help where necessary and see that each child is fully involved. There are always some who will sit back and leave it to others. For children with real difficulties, you may need to define their role. You could turn this work into a competition with prizes for the best group. You might like to ask other teachers or another class to judge it.

Follow-up
In the last chapter of the book, the Iron Man is flown to Australia. Turn to geography at this point and look at a map of Australia, finding Tasmania and the Gulf of Carpentaria. You could link this with maths work in looking at the size of the Space Being. Look at the height of the Hindu Kush; this creature towered even higher. Look at Italy; its head alone was the size of this country while its stomach was the size of Germany.

Read some of Ted Hughes' poetry for children, such as the following:
Meet my folks!
The Earth-Owl and other Moon-People
Nessie the Mannerless Monster.
All are published by Faber and are available in paperback.

The Great Piratical Rumbustification
Margaret Mahy (Dent/Puffin)

'Music flowed like rum, and rum flowed like music.'

Age range
Six to nine.

Setting the scene
Create an area with plenty of room where nautical things can be displayed. If you have oars, sails, sailbags or even a small rubber dinghy, all the better. Floats, shells or mobiles (the type which can be bought in seaside shops) will help add to the seaside atmosphere. Backing paper covered in stars, with the words 'PIRATE PARTY' written across it, will set the scene. Paint could be used to create the flare effect around the words.

Synopsis
This is a book to capture every child's imagination. When Mr Terrapin phones the Mother Goose baby sitting agency, he is somewhat taken aback when Orpheus Clinker arrives to do the job. It is obvious to everyone, especially Alpha, Oliver and Omega, the Terrapins' badly-behaved children, that he is a pirate. As soon as the Terrapins leave, Orpheus lights some flares in the garden which advertise 'Pirate Party' across the sky. Soon the smell of 'Pirate Stew' encourages pirates, neighbours and passers-by to take part in the best rumbustification ever.

Pirate names

Age range
Six to eight.

Group size
Whole class.

What you need
Children sitting informally.

What to do
Discuss some suitable pirate names with the children, such as One-eyed Jack, or names from the book such as Orpheus Clinker or Terrible Crabmeat. Ask the children to make up their own pirate names. Some children might like to use their own names, such as Yo ho ho Rachel, Wooden-leg Watson or Crossbones Wright.

Self-portraits

Age range
Six to nine.

Group size
Individuals.

What you need
Mirrors, large sheets of paper, pencils, paint, brushes, scissors, black sugar paper, white chalk.

What to do
Provide some mirrors so that the children can look at the proportions of their facial features. Make some drawings on the blackboard to help them. Ask each child to draw and paint his face including neck and shoulders. Help the children to mix a suitable skin colour in paint. Cut the faces out and add black sugar paper pirate hats. Add a skull and crossbones in white chalk.

Wonderful words

Age range
Six to nine.

Group size
Whole class.

What you need
Paper, pencils.

Rumbustification

raggle-taggle

Younger Generanium

a peppery parroty party

Hop-and-go-carry-one

What to do
Read the first three chapters of the book. Discuss the word 'Rumbustification'. This is a lovely word for the children to roll around their tongues. Do they know any more words like this? Make a list of these and display them around the room.

Pirate masks

Age range
Seven to nine.

Group size
Children working in pairs.

What you need
Balloons, wallpaper paste, newspaper, liquid detergent, craft knife, paint, brushes, fabric scraps, metal rings.

What to do
Blow up one balloon for every two children, allowing one extra in case of accidents. Tear newspaper into small strips and dip these in paste. Smear the balloons lightly with liquid detergent then cover them completely with the newspaper, the more layers the better. Allow the papier mâché to dry thoroughly (this can take up to two days) then carefully prick the balloons to burst them. Using a craft knife with the teacher's help, carefully cut the papier mâché shapes in half lengthways to give two masks, then paint on pirate faces. Stick on fabric hats, beards, moustaches and ear-rings. Cut out holes for eyes.

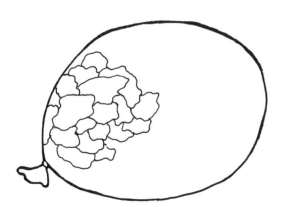

Communications

Age range
Seven to nine.

Group size
Whole class.

What you need
String, card or paper, crayons, paints, stapler, examples of flags and morse code (see pages 117 and 118).

What to do
Discuss how pirates might communicate. They could use morse code and flags (see pages 117 and 118). Tap out SOS in morse code. Make flags from card or paper, staple them on to lengths of string and then suspend them across the classroom. You could also make a cardboard mast and attach strings of flags to the top. Fly a skull and crossbones flag from the mast.

Pirate party

Age range
Six to eight.

Group size
Whole class.

What you need
A good space, musical instruments.

What to do
Re-enact the 'Pirate Party'. Teach the children a simple hornpipe dance. Some children might be able to play a hornpipe tune on the recorder, while others could play the tambourine as Mr Terrapin did. Others could play chime bars to represent the coins falling into the stew pot. Act out the Terrapins' amazement when they find out that their house has been used for pirate purposes.

Follow-up
See if there are any radio or TV broadcasts which fit in with your sea theme. Read lots of sea poems and shanties. Look at *The Puffin Book of Salt Sea Verse*, ed Causley (Puffin). Learn the song 'One Eyed Jack, the Pirate King' from *Poems for 7 Year-Olds and Under*, ed Helen Nicoll (Kestrel) and the poem *The Jumblies* by Edward Lear (Beehive/Grafton). Younger children love the repetitive chorus.

I used *Granny's Garden* (4 Mation Educational Resources) computer game at the same time and the children came up with the idea of inviting the creatures from Granny's garden to the 'Pirate Party'.

The Night-watchmen

Helen Cresswell (Faber/Puffin)

'Henry, listening to the soft stirring of coals in the brazier and the soughing of the wind under stone arches, was for the first time conscious of the charms of the life of a night-watchman.'

Age range
Eight to eleven.

Synopsis
Henry is a little boy recovering from an illness. With time on his hands, he begins to explore and meets with two tramps, Josh and Caleb. They talk of mysterious things: 'ticking', 'Greeneyes' and places called 'Here' and 'There'.

They live in a night-watchman's tent, by a hole surrounded by lamps and signs. In this way they do not attract attention.

They talk of escape by a night train on its way to 'There'. As the Greeneyes close in upon them, Henry becomes involved in arranging their escape and even has a ride on the night train. Lots of mysteries are left unanswered, therefore allowing children plenty of scope to use their imagination.

Setting the scene
Arrange three or four tables together with a gap between them. Cover them with drapes such as old sheets or curtains, pushing the fabric down into the gap to create a hole. Set up a display board with the words *The Night-watchmen*. Make a cardboard signpost and label its arms 'Here, There, and Everywhere'.

Discussion

Age range
Eight to ten.

Group size
Whole class.

What you need
Children sitting informally.

What to do
Read the first three and a bit pages as far as the words 'He made a raft.' Two factors emerge from this: the waiting and the illness. Can the children recollect having had to wait for anything? How did they pass the time?

Now discuss Henry's illness. What sort of illness could have kept Henry in bed for a long time? Point out that the book was first published in 1969 when children would have been kept in bed for a long time with illnesses such as glandular fever. Now, more effective antibiotics have been developed and it would have to be a very serious illness to keep you in bed and off school for a long time.

Collage of characters

Age range
Eight to eleven.

Group size
Whole class, three pairs and individuals.

What you need
Paper, an assortment of fabrics, paints, brushes, craft papers including gummed, foil and tissue-papers, pencils, scissors, adhesive, string, wool, pins.

What to do
Read the first chapter. Re-read the descriptions of Josh and Caleb and discuss them with the children. In what way do their appearances differ? Ask three pairs of children each to make large drawings of Henry, Josh and Caleb.

Josh

Henry

Make the roadworks

Age range
Eight to eleven.

Group size
Whole class and small groups.

What you need
Paint, brushes, paper, white card, adhesive, scissors, red acetate film. Optional: red and white fabric.

What to do
Read chapters two, three and four. Lots of possibilities for language work will emerge here. References to 'ticking' and the night train will lead to discussion. Ask the children to describe what they think the 'ticking'

The children may need to borrow the book to look at descriptions, but encourage them not to copy illustrations. Ask them to look for suitable material for coats, trousers and shoes, as well as wool for beards and string to tie around the waist. If they make tracings of the clothes they have drawn and cut them out, they will have a paper pattern to pin on to the fabric; this takes out the guesswork. Other children can draw and paint the characters on A4 sheets of paper, cut them out and display them with large lettering at the side indicating who they are.

actually is. Discuss roadworks and the red and white huts. Ask whether anyone has spotted one on their road, then ask them to describe it.

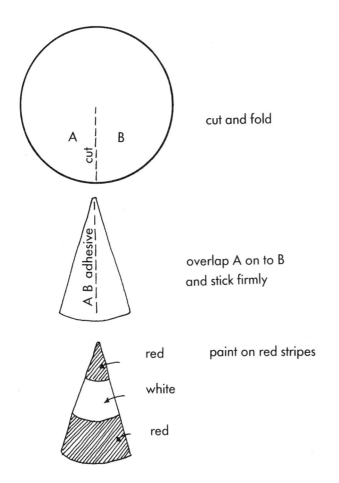

cut and fold

overlap A on to B and stick firmly

paint on red stripes

red

white

red

Divide the class into groups and ask them to make traffic cones. Cut out large circles from white card, then make a cut to the centre, overlap the cut edges and stick them firmly together. Paint on red stripes.

Ask some of the children to make a large free-standing sign saying, 'Danger, men at work' in red lettering. Stress that the lettering must be easy to read. Ask other children to make lamps of the type found by road-works. Encourage them to design their own lamps using card and red acetate film. Display all these around the 'hole' made from the tables.

If you have some red and white fabric, drape it over a box to make the hut.

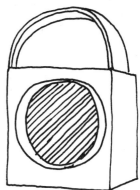

Recipes

Age range
Eight to ten.

Group size
Individuals.

What you need
Paper, pencils, crayons, cookery books.

What to do
Ask the children to write a recipe for a night-watchman's dinner. Show them examples of recipes and cookery books and discuss how they are written. They usually state:
- How many people the recipe is for.
- Ingredients.
- Cooking time and temperature.
- Method of cooking.
- What to eat with it.

Ask the children to illustrate their recipe.

Night train imagery

Age range
Eight to eleven.

Group size
Individuals.

What you need
Paper, pencils.

What to do
Read chapter six which contains wonderful descriptions of the night train. Read these descriptions several times and point out the author's devices, as in 'The wind over the top comes rushing into your mouth like jugfuls of cold water.' This should provide a good basis for children to produce their own word pictures. Discuss how the poems are going to be presented. Illustrations of the night train can be drawn around or under the poem, or drawn and coloured lightly first with the writing on top.

Photofits

Age range
Eight to ten.

Group size
Whole class divided into groups of three.

What you need
Paper cut into equal strips, paper for backing, pencils, crayons.

What to do
Give each child a strip of paper, then divide the class into groups of three. Ask one child in each group to draw the top part of a head with either green eyes or sunglasses. Another child draws the cheeks, nose and upper lip, while the third draws the rest of the mouth, the chin and the top of the neck. Then ask the children to stick the three pieces of paper together on to backing paper to form a face. Ask them to make a written description to accompany this.

Follow-up
Much more display work can be produced. The night train can be drawn and painted and the 'Greeneyes' can be added to the display.

Work could then be done on steam trains or roadworks. The class might be able to go out to look at some roadworks. With younger children, point out that they should not talk to strangers; it might be acceptable in a book, but not in real life.

Fattypuffs and Thinifers
André Maurois (Bodley Head/Puffin)

'A moving staircase, so long that one could not see its end, was rumbling down into the centre of the earth.'

Age range
Eight to eleven.

Synopsis
This book was written in French in 1930, but it is still enjoyed by children today. It is about two brothers, one thin, one fat, who go with their father for a walk one Sunday in the summer. The boys go off climbing and discover a grotto with tunnels and a moving staircase which leads to the world of Fattypuffs and Thinifers where a war ensues between the two kingdoms. Because of their physical make-up, the boys are separated and become part of these two races. All ends well when the boys eventually help them to unite.

Setting the scene
It is important that you consider the children in your class, making sure that you don't have any children with weight problems, as this could lead to difficulties.
   You will need a good collection of books about food and the digestive system, the human body, and a model skeleton if possible. You will need an area suitable for wall display and for displaying card models.

A letter from Thinifer

Age range
Eight to eleven.

Group size
Whole class and individual work.

What you need
Paper, pencils, crayons.

What to do
After introducing the children to the first part of the story, ask them to write a letter to a friend describing what it would be like to be a Thinifer. Read the chapters 'The Thiniport Line' and 'The Thinifers at Home' and pick out the descriptions of the Thinifers and Fattypuffs. This is a good opportunity to look at the correct layout for a letter. The children will need to make up a Thinifer address. They can accompany their letter with illustrations.

Anatomy and physiology

Age range
Nine to eleven.

Group size
Whole class.

What you need
Model skeleton, books on the human body.

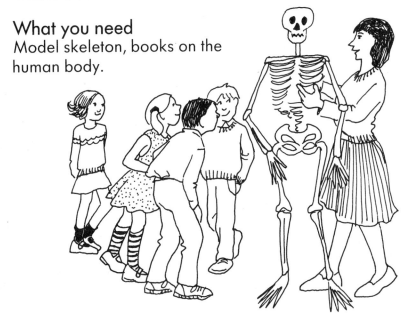

What to do
This book gives an opportunity to study both health and fitness and the human body.

The topic of health and fitness could be divided into diet, teeth, skin, physical fitness and hygiene. PE lessons could also be involved here.

Look at the workings of the heart, lungs and muscles. You may also want to look at the bones of the body, using a model skeleton. This, of course, is a very detailed area, and could give rise to a whole term's work in itself.

Model Thinifers

Age range
Eight to eleven.

Group size
Individuals or small groups.

What you need
Card, art straws, pencils, paint, brushes, adhesive, scissors, fabric, thread.

What to do
Look at the illustration in chapter three, 'The Thiniport Line' of the Thinifers keeping fit. Ask the children to make some drawings on card of Thinifers doing some of these activities. Paint the figures or stick on pieces of fabric for clothes, then cut them out. Suspend some from the ceiling and mount others on the walls with cardboard tabs behind them to make them appear three-dimensional. Make models of Thinifers from card and use art straws to make swings and other apparatus. Display them standing on various surfaces: I had one Thinifer doing a balance on top of the blackboard. Well-displayed these can look very amusing.

You are what you eat

Age range
Eight to eleven.

Group size
Individuals.

What you need
Copies of the food chart for each member of your class (see page 119), books about diet and nutrition.

What to do
Ask the children to take home the chart every night for a week and record the types of food and drink they have consumed. The results of this can be translated into a large graph. Ask them to cut out pictures of food from magazines and add them to the graph to give it colour. Discuss the results with the children and decide whether a good balance of food is being eaten.

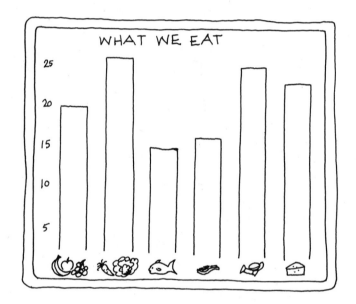

I'm not a Thinifer . . .

Age range
Eight to eleven.

Group size
Whole class or groups.

What you need
Large sheets of paper, pencils, paint, brushes, scissors, fabric, adhesive.

What to do
Lay a large sheet of paper on the floor, ask one child to lay down on it and another to draw round their outline. Use the drawing as a pattern by cutting it up and placing the various parts on different kinds of fabric then cutting out the head, legs, arms, T-shirt, trousers or skirt and feet. Reassemble the parts and stick them on to another large sheet of paper.

Make a drawing of Mr Dulcifer saying 'You are a half-wit and a nincompoop!' to display beside it. The picture of the child in your class could be saying, 'I'll eat all the correct food. I'm not a Thinifer and I'm certainly not a Fattypuff'.

Poetical people

Age range
Eight to eleven.

Group size
Whole class, then individual work.

What you need
Paper, pencils.

What to do
Read the various descriptions of the Fattypuffs and the Thinifers. Ask the children to write a word picture about them, accompanied by illustrations.

Predict an ending

Age range
Eight to eleven.

Group size
Individuals.

What you need
Paper, pencils.

What to do
Read up to the end of chapter eleven. Ask the children to write an account of how they think the story will end. Remind them about the boy's father who has been waiting for them. How long have they been away? This could lead to some amusing writing which the children could read to each other. After this read the end of the book to them.

The Secret World of Polly Flint
Helen Cresswell (Faber/Puffin)

'There was the world of every day, of clocks ticking and rain falling . . . And there was her own, secret world, where she reigned over her own kingdom.'

Age range
Nine to eleven.

Synopsis
This is a magical tale, set in Wellow, a north Nottinghamshire village. Below Wellow is a lost village which has slipped the 'net of time'. Taken with it are time gypsies who, at certain times, can move between the two worlds. Polly has magical powers which enable her to see them. The time gypsies are not allowed to eat earthly food otherwise they forfeit their gift of slipping the net of time. This is what has happened to Old Mazy who ate food given to him by a local farmer. He becomes known as the Catcher and tries to trap the rest of the gypsies in the net of time. With her magical powers, Polly is able to help the time gypsies and Old Mazy, and in doing so briefly visits their kingdom situated below Rufford Park.

Setting the scene
A large wall area is necessary, covered from floor to ceiling with backing paper. Divide the area in half horizontally. Make the lower half into Polly's secret world and the upper half the real world. There is a map in the book which shows the layout of the park, and pamphlets, postcards and information about wildlife are available from Rufford Country Park itself (see 'Study of water birds' activity for the address). If you do not live in the Nottinghamshire area, you may have a similar park nearby which has lakes, woods and water birds which could provide similar inspiration.

Start your display

Age range
Nine to eleven.

Group size
Groups or whole class.

What you need
Assorted art media such as paper, card, adhesive, paint, brushes, foil, art straws, fabric, netting and tissue-paper.

What to do
Make a collage of the two worlds of Polly Flint. Ask the children to draw the time gypsies, Polly, Boz/Baggins and the Catcher/Old Mazy. Make Polly and the Catcher much larger than the other characters. Place the Catcher so that he stands above the lost village. If you have some netting or net-like material, drape this from Old Mazy's hand, so that it falls into the secret world, symbolising the 'net of time'. Use art straws and foil to create stalactites and stalagmites in the world below.

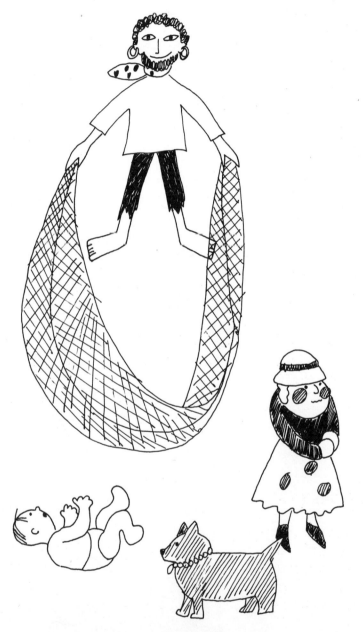

Study of water birds

Age range
Nine to eleven.

Group size
Whole class.

What you need
Rufford Park's water birds sheet available from Rufford Country Park, Rufford Mill, Ollerton, Nottinghamshire; tel: 0623 - 824153; books on birds, copies of the chart on page 120.

What to do
Ask the children to make a study of water birds. Provide them with a chart (see page 120). This will help ensure that they have a guide-line for the information required. Ask the children to bring in any bird books they might have at home. A class visit to see some water birds would be helpful, if only to a small pond.

Soft toy

Age range
Nine to eleven.

Group size
Individuals.

What you need
Paper, pencils, scissors, felt, pins, needle, thread, clean old tights, copy of template on page 121.

What to do
Using the template on page 121 for reference, draw and cut out a paper pattern for a duck. Stitch the beak, eyes and feet in place, then pin the pieces of the body wrong sides together. Sew along the edges in a small running stitch, leaving a small gap for stuffing. Cut up old pairs of tights into very small pieces, fill the duck with them and then sew up the gap.

Woodpecker mobiles

Age range
Nine to eleven.

Group size
Individuals.

What you need
Two pieces of thin card for each person, pencils, scissors, cardboard tubes, adhesive, stapler, felt-tipped pens, thread.

What to do
Get the children to fold the pieces of card in half, draw on the head and body of a woodpecker (see figure 1) and cut them out. Apply adhesive to the underside of the

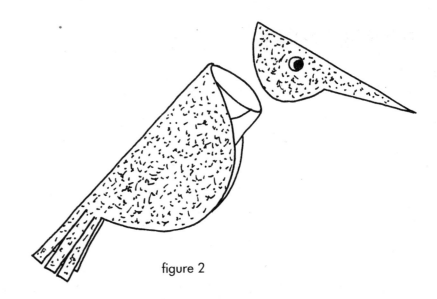

figure 2

body and then stick it to the cardboard tube. Staple the head to the top of the tube (see figure 2). The woodpeckers can then be decorated with brightly-coloured felt-tipped pens and suspended from the ceiling with thread.

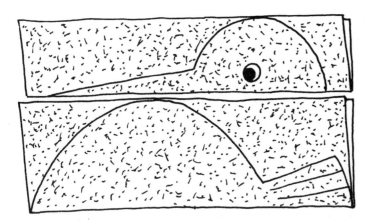

figure 1

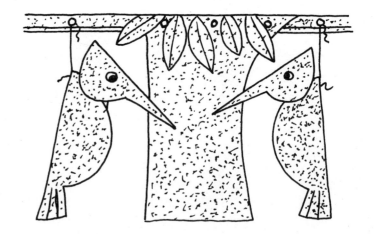

Wildlife work

Age range
Nine to eleven.

Group size
Whole class and individual work.

What you need
Books about wildlife, pencils, paper, flower press.

What to do
Make a study of the insects, plant life and animals which could be found in Rufford Park or a similar country park. Use the environment around the school if some of these plants and creatures are in evidence.

Encourage the children to make rough notes from several books, to write up information in their own words and to include the author and the title of all books used.

Ask the children to make a small collection of wild flowers and leaves, press them, mount them on to paper and label them. Remember to stress how precious wild flowers are and insist that one sample is enough. They will not be allowed to take any specimens from country parks.

Map work

Age range
Nine to eleven.

Group size
Whole class and individual work.

What you need
Plan of Rufford Park (a map is available from the park but the plan inside the book will do), centimetre squared paper, pencils, felt-tipped pens, paper, sugar paper.

What to do
As a class, decide how many kilometres the park covers. Decide also on a scale, ie so many centimetres equals so many kilometres. Ask the children to draw the map on squared paper.

Follow-up
Visit a park with a nature trail, then make a display of photographs, sketches and written work. These could be incorporated into a class book or individual folders.

The Bongleweed

Helen Cresswell (Faber/Puffin)

'The Bongleweed was uncontainable in its urge to spread, climb, put forth.'

Age range
Eight to eleven.

Synopsis
When the head gardener's daughter, Becky, takes some strange seeds from the greenhouse and gives them to Jason, the nephew of her father's employer, she does not realise what the full extent of the outcome will be. Planted in her mother's little garden, the strange plant grows rapidly, spreading and covering, blooming, talking and, in the end, communicating with Becky. Eventually her father has to make a tremendous decision, either he must hand in his notice or somehow the plant must go. However, nature takes its course, the Bongleweed dies and life returns to normal.

Setting the scene
Draw and cut out giant beanstalks and display them so that they touch the classroom ceiling. Make some huge leaves from tissue and crêpe paper. Collect together books about plants, Kew gardens, and other botanical gardens. Collect seed trays and assorted seeds.

Make the Bongleweed

Age range
Eight to eleven.

Group size
Whole class.

What you need
Tissue or crêpe paper, scissors, string or garden wire, sugar paper in various shades of green, red and yellow, adhesive.

What to do
Read the class the first few chapters of *The Bongleweed* to set the scene, then ask the children to make huge leaves and gigantic red and yellow flowers out of the sugar paper. Use garden wire or string to trail them liberally across the classroom ceiling, and along corridors and cloakrooms. Trail some of it around doorways and windows. Wind strips of green crêpe paper around the wire or string and staple the leaves and flowers on to it. Cut out ten large leaves and on each one put brightly coloured letters to spell out the word 'Bongleweed'.

Pictures and writing

Age range
Eight to eleven.

Group size
Individuals.

What you need
Paper, pencils, crayons, paints, brushes.

What to do
Read the book thoroughly yourself, then pick out some examples of good writing, eg 'He *is* like forced rhubarb. With spectacles' or 'On a wild night with a raggedy wind'. Ask the children to draw or paint the images that come to mind, then ask them to make up some descriptions themselves using similes, metaphors and good adjectives to describe people and things. The moon is a wonderful example; in chapter 12 there are some superb descriptions of moonlight, such as 'The moon . . . hanging over Pew like a giant circular Chinese lantern'. In this chapter there are also descriptions of plants and people in moonlight.

Growing seeds

Age range
Eight to eleven.

Group size
Children working in groups of two, three or four.

What you need
Seed trays, jars, blotting paper, seeds, beans, plant pots, compost, various soil types, paper, pencils.

What to do
Divide the class into small groups. Get each group to carry out experiments with seed growth, using different methods of germination and watering and different amounts of sunlight. Explain to the class that in order to ensure that the test is fair they will all use the same type of seeds. At the same time, grow mustard and cress and sprout beans in jars with damp blotting paper. If you have a bean sprouter, this is wonderful for demonstrating rapid growth. Morning glory seeds germinate well and the growth from these is rapid. Ask the children to measure the daily growth and plot the information on a graph. Record the progress of the experiment under headings such as: 'Experiment to show . . .'; 'Apparatus used'; 'What we did'; 'What happened' and 'Conclusion'.

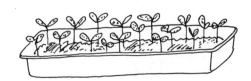

Weedy words

Age range
Eight to eleven.

Group size
Individuals, small groups to display work.

What you need
Jotter, paper, pencils, crayons, green paper.

What to do
Ask the children to write a word picture about the Bongleweed. When they are finished and any corrections have been made, ask the children to write them out on large leaf or flower shapes, then display them grouped together attached to stalks. The following work was done by ten-and eleven-year-olds.

Bongleweed, Bongleweed.
Where are you going?
I'm going to grow up the big brick wall,
And in the graveyard, up houses, down chimneys, down drainpipes.
I will spoil the children's long large kites in the sky.
.... He had been run over by a car,
They had a little funeral,
The whole town came to see the Bongleweed,
And they all cried out loud!
The Bongleweed will never be seen again.

Not last night but the night before,
I planted some seeds outside my door,
It grew in the moonlight,
It grew in the day,
It grew up my house,
It went all the way,
It spread all over the garden,
All over next doors too,
I could not stop it growing,
It just grew and grew and grew.
It went up into the street that night
It covered up some cars,
It climbed upon a lamp post,
Nearly touching all the stars,
This mystery just had to be solved
I could not believe my eyes,
But when I chopped it down that night
I knew I heard its cries.

The ten-year-old boy who wrote this poem accompanied it with leaves and stalks which entwined around his writing and he added bright red flowers in appropriate spaces. He mounted his work on a flower shape and carefully added a centre made from crêpe and tissue-paper.

The growing Bongleweed of Kirkby
Must have been a million metres long.
It grew from the garden of Tommy Jones,
And over the greenhouse patch,
Where it smashed the daisies as flat as a pancakes.
(And even flatter than that)

It grew over the wall and into the road,
Where ten cars were crushed like grapes.
It grew to the spire of St. Thomas' church but still
it kept growing.

The Bongleweed must have now grown a billion metres.
I think even much longer than that.

Next it came to a cemetery and knocked down
the memorial and crushed the roses as flat
as Italian Pizzas.

Then to our school came the grotesque weed.
It went to the roof where it knocked the bell,
It broke down the doors and the windows fell out.

Bongleweed, Bongleweed please go away.
But he's here to stay.

Write away

Age range
Eight to eleven.

Group size
Whole class and individuals.

What you need
A copy of *Treasure Chest for Teachers* (The Teacher Publishing Co Ltd), writing paper, pens.

What to do
Ask the children to write away for some information about plants from places such as the Royal Botanic Gardens, Kew, Richmond, Surrey TW9 3AB or the Forestry Commission, 231 Corstorphine Road, Edinburgh, EH12 7AT. This helps reinforce layout and the style of letters. The children are always thrilled when the secretary brings them the post! Information can be used for individual's folders or for display.

Follow-up
Take the children to visit a garden. Plant some trees or bulbs at school.

'The Librarian and the Robbers'
from The Great Piratical Rumbustification, Margaret Mahy (Dent-Puffin)

'"Pulverized by literature," thought Miss Laburnum, "The ideal way for a librarian to die."'

Age range
Seven to eleven.

Synopsis
When Miss Serena Laburnum is captured by a band of inefficient robbers, they do not realise that their days of lawlessness are nearly at an end. She has been staying with friends who have the 'Raging Measles' and she passes it on to the robbers. To entertain them whilst they are ill, she reads them stories and when they are well they let her go. After Serena files the Robber Chief in the library under his surname and then takes him out on her library membership card, and after an earthquake which nearly buries her in library books, the robbers decide to reform. Serena Laburnum marries the Robber Chief and becomes Mrs Loveday.

Setting the scene
Some of the work can be done in the classroom and some in the library. You may wish to display some work but much is of an oral or note-taking nature.

Alphabetical order

Age range
Nine to eleven.

Group size
Groups of no more than eight children.

What you need
Telephone directories including the *Yellow Pages*, prepared work cards, paper, pencils, white index cards with different words on them.

What to do
In order to explain the use of alphabetical order make work cards which the children can use to look up names and addresses to find out telephone numbers. If you choose popular surnames, the children will soon become aware that the names are entered in strict alphabetical order.

When making work cards using the *Yellow Pages*, put these in the form of a problem, eg 'My car has broken down. Find a suitable telephone number to ring to help me with this problem.' or 'I want to go out for a meal at a Chinese restaurant. Where can I go?'. This involves more than just using simple alphabetical order as the children have to think what categories to look under. This is valuable training for finding library books and using catalogue and computer lists. Point out that in the story it says 'Alphabetical order is a habit with librarians'.

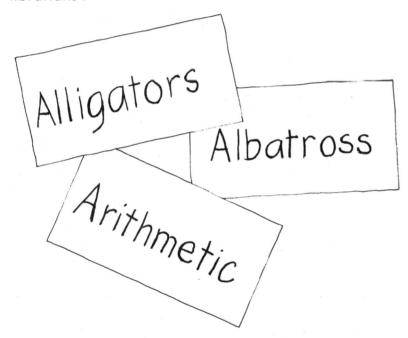

Alternatively, give the children a number of cards on which you have written different words and ask them to put them in alphabetical order. With younger children simple words beginning with different letters are the best to start with. With older children use words starting with the same letter, eg alligators, albatross, arithmetic.

Finding fiction

Age range
Eight to eleven.

Group size
Whole class.

What you need
Access to a school or public library.

What to do
Look at the way in which Serena files the Robber Chief in alphabetical order. Then look at the way in which fiction books are arranged on the shelves in libraries. Why do you need an arrangement? Why couldn't you arrange the books in title order? Children often have favourite authors and might want to see if anything else has been written by that person, so if all the author's works are put together they can easily see what else is available. If you have a school library you might like to devise some work cards or quizzes to do with alphabetical arrangement. Visit a local library and ask the children's librarian for project ideas.

Libraries

Age range
Nine to eleven.

Group size
Whole class.

What you need
Access to a library.

What to do
Your school library might be arranged by colour coding or by the Dewey decimal system. The Dewey system really is the best arrangement, even with younger children. Each subject is given a separate number and the books are arranged from 000 to 999. Individual books are then identified by the number after the decimal point. When using colour coding you are limiting yourself to generalising, but the Dewey system, because of its decimal nature is specific and allows for the addition of new subjects. You need not go beyond the two decimal points. With older juniors, this might provide a practical introduction to learning about decimals.

Whichever arrangement you use, the children should understand it and be able to find books for themselves or help from adults should be available. For a school library to work efficiently there should be a teacher responsible for it who works closely with the local library or county library system. It would be even better if parents could staff the library on a rota system so that it could be fully operational.

Discuss with the children why non-fiction needs to be arranged differently to fiction. To do this you might need to discuss what is fiction, and what is non-fiction. Explain how factual books need to be arranged in subject order and ask the children for examples of subjects. For example, you would want to find together all books on pets, trees, maths, countries etc. Guide the children around your library shelves.

If you have very large books do you have an oversize section?

Finally, you should have a list or a catalogue of all main subjects arranged in alphabetical order and the children should understand how to look up a subject. Alongside the subject should be the Dewey number – or if colour coded, the colour should be entered. The children should be encouraged to find their own books whenever possible.

Reference books

Age range
Nine to eleven.

Group size
Whole class.

What you need
Encyclopaedias, dictionaries and other reference books.

What to do
Look at the alphabetical arrangement used inside encyclopaedias. Larger sets have a volume index which you should show the children. This is also arranged in alphabetical order and gives the volume number where information is to be found, the page number and sometimes the column number.

Look at a dictionary where again strict alphabetical order is used. Larger ones give lots of information about the words, pronunciation and origin. With older children you might like to look at some words in detail.

If you have a thesaurus, the children will have help at hand when you ask them to use different words in their stories.

Look at trade directories. These are available in libraries – you might be able to obtain a supply of out-of-date ones. Older children will find the arrangement of information very interesting.

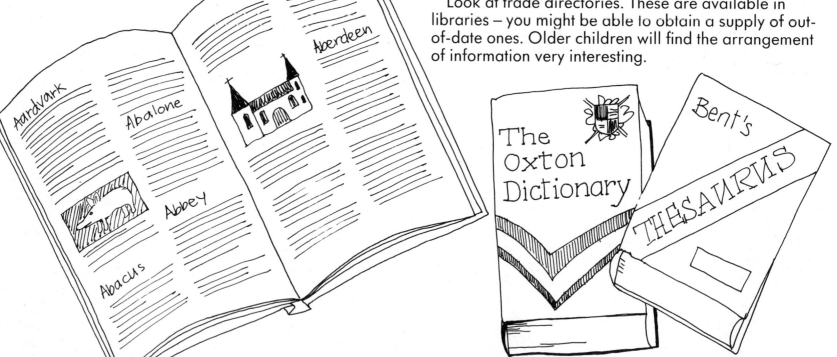

The Siege of White Deer Park
Colin Dann (Hutchinson/Beaver)

'Tawny Owl . . . opened one eye . . . . A huge face, with eyes glinting in the moonlight like live coals, stared up at him.'

Age range
Eight to eleven.

Synopsis
White Deer Park is a nature reserve, home for many animals including some survivors from Farthing Wood who have sworn to be faithful and helpful to each other. Suddenly, their lives are totally disrupted by an animal so cunning, stealthy and deadly, that they seem powerless to overcome this savage killer. At first they are unaware of the sort of creature he is, but eventually they find out that he is a large wild cat. Even the rangers in the reserve seem powerless to overcome his treachery. However, nature comes to their rescue and finally their security and peace of mind returns once more.

Setting the scene
Set up a display board and add the words 'What Sort of Creature?'. Have a supply of large cat posters available and put one or two up on the board but don't make any further comment. Have a variety of animal books on display and collect animal pictures which will be suitable for display. These should include badgers, rabbits, tawny owls, herons, foxes, adders, moles, deer, hares and weasels. Books of poems about animals are also useful for ideas.

WHAT SORT OF CREATURE ?

Wanted poster

Age range
Eight to eleven.

Group size
Whole class, then individual work.

What you need
Paper, pencils, crayons.

What to do
Read the first chapter, 'What Sort of Creature?'. Now ask the children to create a 'Wanted' poster. The creature should be named, a brief description given, and a good drawing made. You will find that most children will immediately think of cats because of the pictures you have displayed. Some, however, will draw other creatures, perhaps even monsters.

This animal is extremely dangerous and should be approached with extreme caution

Word creature

Age range
Eight to eleven.

Group size
Individuals.

What you need
Paper, pencils, crayons.

What to do
Ask the children to write a word picture about the creature. By now through discussion, the class will probably have come to the conclusion that it is a cat, so you can discuss the types of words which will convey how the creature looks, how it thinks, how it moves and hunts. Discuss the sounds its movements make. What will its paws be doing? What will its claws, nose, mouth, ears and eyes be doing? A good word picture should emerge from this. Write up and illustrate the work suitably. These two activities will complete your display 'What Sort of Creature?'.

fierce   snarling

stealthy   cruel   roar

vicious   cunning

growling   savage

Animal information

Age range
Eight to eleven.

Group size
Whole class, then individual work.

What you need
A collection of books on snakes and foxes, pencils, paper.

FOX FACTS
1. Baby foxes are called cubs.
2. A fox lives in a hole called an earth.
3. A female fox is called a vixen.
4. A fox's tail is called a brush.

What to do
Read the first six chapters of the book so that the children are familiar with some more of the creatures, then introduce the idea of using books for information. First look at factual books, their layout, indexes and contents pages. Stress that the children should not write down anything that they do not understand, or copy directly.

Now ask them to find out ten facts about foxes or snakes. They should use as many books as possible to obtain information and use the school library if you have one. Stress that information will not just be in specific books but that they will have to look in general animal books. They will, therefore, have to use the index. Finally ask them to write down the author, title and publisher for each book they have used.

Snake shapes and poems

Age range
Eight to eleven.

Group size
Whole class.

What you need
Paper, pencils, copies of the snake outline on page 122 on A4 paper.

What to do
Make a list of words to describe a snake and look at alliteration. A lot of snake words include the letter 'S', but do try to avoid 'slimy'. Hissing, slithery etc, are appropriate. Read 'The Serpent' by Theodore Roethke, in *A Children's Zoo* compiled by Julia Watson (Armada Lions). Ask the children to write a poem or word picture describing a snake, then copy it out on to the snake shape you have provided.

Figures of speech

Age range
Eight to nine.

Group size
Whole class, then individual work.

What you need
Paper, pencils, crayons.

What to do
Read the chapter 'Trouble in Store', drawing the children's attention to the phrase 'Now don't get in a coil'.

Here is a superb opportunity for language work – discuss such expressions as 'Keep your hair on', 'Don't get your knickers in a twist' and 'Keep your shirt on'. Ask the children to write down one of these expressions and illustrate it. After you have looked at these together and discussed them, ask the children to think of expressions which could be applied to animals. They will come up with things such as 'Don't hop your head off' for kangaroos or 'Don't lose your trunk' for elephants.

Wild cat frieze

Age range
Eight to eleven.

Group size
Whole class or small groups.

What you need
Photographs of wild cats for reference, pencils, stiff frieze paper for the background, paints, brushes, brown leather scraps, scissors, adhesive.

What to do
Study the photographs, then draw a large outline of a wild cat on the background paper. Paint a forest background behind the wild cat. Fill in the animal's outline with a golden brown colour.

Cut the leather scraps into elongated triangles and narrow strips, and try them out in various positions within the animal's outline until it resembles a wild cat's coat. Refer closely to the photographs to see which way the markings lie.

Cut out a narrow oval of paper for an eye, circles for the ears and nose and short fat leather stripes for the tail. When you have a realistic looking wild cat, stick each of the scraps in place individually.

Follow-up
Children could visit a rare breeds centre, deer park or zoo.

The Hobbit
J R R Tolkien (Unwin Hyman Ltd)

'Gandalf! If you had heard only a quarter of what I have heard about him . . . you would be prepared for any sort of remarkable tale.'

Age range
Nine to eleven.

Synopsis
The Hobbit is a book you either find entrancing and which leads you on to read *The Lord of the Rings* or one which you find a nonsense. It is a book that brings out the very best of children's art and written work. The hobbit, Bilbo Baggins, is suddenly called upon by Gandalf the wizard, to undertake an adventure of the greatest daring and danger. With a band of dwarfs he reluctantly sets forth to find the stolen treasure which the dragon Smaug jealously guards. Many adventures befall them including a desperate journey through Mirkwood and meetings with giant spiders, the sinister Gollum and trolls, elves and goblins along the way. *The Hobbit* would leave you almost exhausted were it not lightened with happy moments, and of course it has a successful ending. It is a book packed with opportunities to motivate any class.

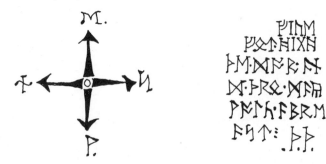

Setting the scene
If possible leave all the display boards in the classroom and corridor free for this project, or leave a large area for display.

If you have a long board, use this to illustrate the journey of the hobbit, plotting its progress through paintings, drawings and written work. Mark in the points of the compass where the journey begins and use runes as shown in the map in the book to indicate the directions taken. Leave room to hang things from the ceiling. If you have another long board, use this for Smaug the dragon; this can be your real starting point. Push a long row of desks together so that all the children can work on Smaug at once.

Smaug the dragon

Age range
Nine to eleven.

Group size
Whole class.

What you need
Frieze paper, pencils, adhesive, cardboard egg boxes, scissors, adhesive, fabric scraps, polystyrene chips, tissue-paper, paints, brushes, stapler, collage materials.

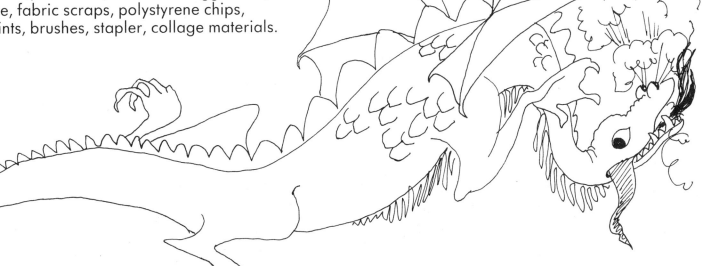

everyone to be able to have a hand in its making. Give the dragon's skin texture by using cardboard egg boxes cut into individual segments, polystyrene chips and

What to do
Before beginning to read the book to the children, explain that a terrible dragon is involved. You could read part of the chapter 'Inside Information' in which Smaug is described as a 'vast red – golden dragon' or you could ask the children to imagine what Smaug is going to look like. Take a long roll of frieze paper and draw an outline of a huge dragon, large enough for

rolled up tissue-paper. If you have read the description to the children they will make him a red, golden dragon. If not, you will probably find that the children colour him green.

Display Smaug by stapling him to the wall. Ask the children to make red and yellow tissue-paper flames to emerge from his nostrils and sharp claws from collage materials.

As an alternative, make a three-dimensional model from boxes.

Drawings of dwarfs

Age range
Nine to eleven.

Group size
Group of 14 children.

What you need
White paper, pencils, paint, brushes, scissors, card.

What to do
After reading the description of the dwarfs in the first chapter, 'An Unexpected Party', ask the children to draw and paint the dwarfs and Bilbo Baggins. The dwarfs are called: Dori, Nori, Bifur, Bofur, Bombur, Kili, Fili, Ori, Oin, Gloin, Thorin, Balin and Dwalin (13 in all). Cut them out, leaving a thin border of white all the way round and mount them on the display at the beginning of the journey. Label them with their names. You might have trouble remembering the dwarfs' names, but the children will have no difficulty! Cut an arrow from card and mark it 'JOURNEY BEGINS'.

Trolls

Age range
Nine to eleven.

Group size
Whole class.

What you need
Pencils, paper, paint, brushes, collage materials, adhesive.

What to do
Read the chapter 'Roast Mutton' and then get the children to add a painting or collage to the journey board showing the wicked trolls. The text also mentions 'old castles with an evil look', so you might like to ask one child to draw a suitable castle for the display.

Discuss the trolls' language. How has the author made their speech sound rough and uncouth? Ask the children to write a little dialogue as though they were trolls.

Gollum

Age range
Nine to eleven.

Group size
Whole class and individual work.

What you need
Paper, pencils, sugar paper, felt-tipped pens.

What to do
Read 'A Short Rest', 'Over Hill and Under Hill' and 'Riddles in the Dark' and mark these events on your map. The marvellous description and strange speech of Gollum is sure to motivate every single child. These chapters introduce the power of the ring and convey evil and the children will feel nervous for Bilbo. The riddles that Bilbo and Gollum ask each other will become important to the class and the children will try to supply the answers. Ask the children to write a word picture about Gollum using some of Tolkien's descriptions and some of their own words to convey this creature.

Gollum

Gollum lives in the roots of the mountain,
Gollum is slimey and as dark as darkness-s-sss,
Gollum travels on a lake without a fountain,
What's in his pockets -esss,
There must be a mes-s-s,
Probably bones, teeth and shells-s,
Where did he get them?
From underground well-s?
Where did he come from ?
The goblins don't know.

Chorus

Gollum is not kind,
He has an evil mind,
He grabs poor goblins by the scruff of their neck.

Encourage Gollum to speak in their poetry. You might find that these word pictures are longer than usual. This is one of six verses written by an 11-year-old boy.

This was written out on a very large sheet of paper with a drawing of Gollum in the centre. You can then make a class book out of the finished results.

Wall hanging

Age range
Nine to eleven.

Group size
Class divided into groups.

What you need
Large piece of hemmed hessian, scissors, felt, PVA adhesive, fabric scraps, red raffia, sewing threads, needles, knitting yarn, wooden batten, A4 paper, pencils.

What to do
Read the chapter 'Out of the Frying-Pan into the Fire'. Organise one group of children to make a wall hanging, using a large piece of hemmed hessian as a background. Cut out fir trees from felt in different sizes and shades of green, then stick them on to the hessian. Cut dwarfs from scraps of fabric and stick them in front of the trees. Use red raffia to create a flame effect and stick it on, then ask some of the children to embroider flames in yellow thread between the pieces of raffia. Cut out eyes for the wolves from felt, using yellow for the background and brown for the pupils. Cut out triangular noses. Stick the eyes and the noses here and there between the flames. Stitch on some ears for the wolves in chain stitch (see figure 1).

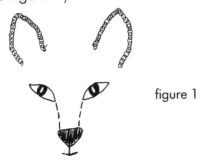

figure 1

To indicate the sky, stitch some lines in running stitch, then stitch grasses in different greens using varying thicknesses of threads or knitting yarns to add interest. Stretch the hessian over a wooden batten at the top and hang it on the wall.

Ask the rest of the class to draw a large outline of a tree on A4 paper and either copy the goblin's song in the shape it appears in the book or make up and illustrate a song of their own.

Mirkwood and the spiders

Age range
Nine to eleven.

Group size
Whole class.

What you need
Paper, stapler, black knitting yarn, string or fishing wire, paints, sequins, needle and cotton, black sugar paper, scissors, adhesive, tissue-paper, glitter.

What to do
Read the chapter 'Queer Lodgings' and mark the events on your map. Then read 'Flies and Spiders'. Discuss the description of the entrance to Mirkwood. Mirkwood could be marked on your journey map with paper trees folded down the middle so that when stapled on to the board they will stand out.

Start making the wood above your head, using as much knitting yarn and string as you can, to create a mish-mash of cobwebs, dangling things and branches hanging from the ceiling. Thread in sequins here and there to create eyes.

Cut out spiders from black sugar paper and cut out holes for the eyes and patterns on the body, then stick coloured tissue-paper behind the cut-outs. Decorate the spiders with glitter. Ask the children to devise a system of levers and pulleys so that the spiders are suspended and move up and down when the door is opened and closed. Be prepared for the expression on any visitors' faces!

Hobbit news

Age range
Nine to eleven.

Group size
Individual jobs.

What you need
Tape recorder, paper, pencils, musical instruments.

What to do
Read to the end of the book and mark all the rest of the journey on your map. Try to make some of it three-dimensional.

The children can then create a news programme:

'Hobbit News'. Ask them to make up a jingle, using their own tune or a tune they know. 'Have you heard the Hobbit News?' to the tune 'Have you seen the Muffin Man?' works very nicely. Other children can be involved working out an accompaniment on recorders, cymbals and drums.

Cast the parts of Bilbo, Gandalf, the dwarfs and the Elven king. Cast the parts of the interviewers. You will need a weather forecaster who can make a map of Wilderland and discuss the weather on the journey. You will also need passers-by, news-readers etc. The programme you make can be radio-style if taped, or television-style if you have access to a video camera. This can produce wonderful drama. The children become so involved with the story of *The Hobbit* that they slip readily into their roles. Even shy children can take part as musicians or technicians.

Follow-up
Maths work on scale, directions and angles can be incorporated. Geographical work can also be introduced by relating the Wilderland map to Ordnance

Survey maps of local areas. After reading the chapter about barrels, science work could be done about floating. Ideas are endless and you may need to set aside a whole term to do justice to this project.

The Wheel on the School
Meindert DeJong (Lutterworth Press/ Puffin)

'Look for a wagon wheel where one is and where one isn't; where one could be and where one couldn't possibly be?'

Age range
Eight to eleven.

Synopsis
This is a story about the children of a small school in Shora, a fishing village on the North Sea coast of Friesland. Shora is positioned next to a dike. Only six of the children in the village are of school age and only one of them is a girl. Because of her enthusiasm the children become very interested in the storks that used to build their nests in Shora. They did so long ago when there were trees and shelter. The children decide they need a wheel placed on the roof of their school to attract the storks back. It is a story of their endeavours and the adventures which befall them as they struggle to find a wheel. In the end they find a wheel, the storks return and the story ends happily.

Setting the scene
You need a good map of Holland and a world map so that you can look at Africa in relation to Holland. Books about Holland and its people would also be useful, and pictures of windmills, bridges and storks. Other Dutch story books such as *Hans Brinker, or the Silver Skates*, Dodge (Puffin) and *The Cow Who Fell in the Canal*, Krasilovsky and Spier (Puffin) would also be of interest.

Also collect pictures of things which are associated with Holland such as bulbs, cheeses and clogs. Don't forget the importance of the fishing and diamond industries. Ask the children if they have any items from Holland such as wooden clogs, model windmills or spoons.

Writing letters

Age range
Eight to eleven.

Group size
Individual to write letter, whole class to receive reply.

What you need
School headed notepaper, envelopes, pencils, pens.

The Netherlands Tourist Office
Egginton House
25-28 Buckingham Gate
London SW1 E6LD

Dear Sir,
Our class is

Class 4
St. Johns C.P. School
Smith Lane
Littlefield
Co. Durham

HOLIDAYS IN HOLLAND

What to do
Ask one of the children to draft a letter to the Netherlands Tourist Office at Egginton House, 25-28 Buckingham Gate, London SW1 E6LD, explaining that the class would like any free information that might be available. It is exciting for the children to receive a reply. If you are lucky you might get some interesting photographs to include in your displays.

Atlas work

Age range
Eight to ten.

Group size
Individuals.

What you need
A set of atlases, large maps, pictures of canals and dikes.

What to do
Ask the children to find the Netherlands in their atlases. Discuss the various words applied to the country and its people, eg Holland, the Netherlands, the Dutch, as this can prove confusing. Look for Friesland and its northern shores. Try to find Shora on the map to see if it is a real or fictional village.

   This offers a useful opportunity to teach the children how to use an index and how to read map references.

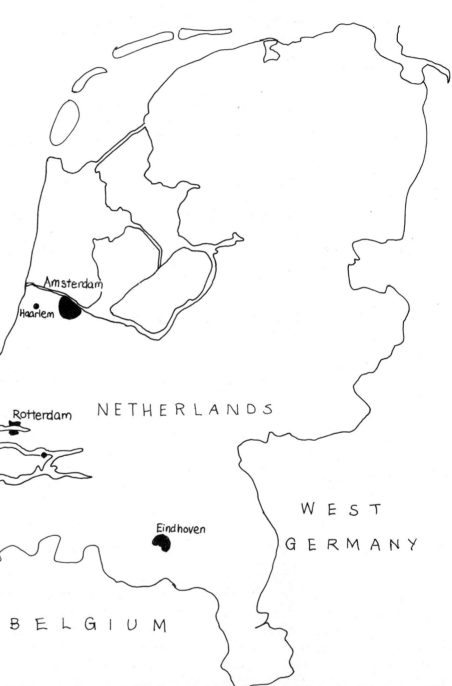

Dikes and polders

Age range
Eight to eleven.

Group size
Individuals.

What you need
Books about Holland.

What to do

Explain to the children about the amazing geography of Holland. Almost one third of the land is below sea level. In order to keep the sea out, a vast system of earth banks called dikes hold back the water and help drain the land. It is kept from reverting to marsh land by being constantly pumped. All the windmills you see in Holland were originally made for this purpose, but nowadays electric pumps are also used. There are little canals every 50 metres or so. Fields reclaimed from the sea are called polders. Ask the children to find pictures in books and find out further information.

All about storks

Age range
Eight to ten.

Group size
Whole class and individual or group work.

What you need
Books and pictures about storks, copies of a world map.

What to do
Look at the life history of a stork and compare what you find out with Lina's discoveries in the first chapter.

Read chapter three 'Wagon Wheel' and the teacher's description of the storks in Africa. Compare the position of Holland in relation to Africa. The children could plot on a world map the route the storks might take.

You might also like to compare the stork with a bird which migrates from the Arctic to spend winter in Britain and ask the children to plot its flight.

Windmills

Age range
Eight to eleven.

Group size
Small groups of two to four children.

What you need
Empty washing-up liquid bottles, cardboard, paper clips, elastic bands, drawing pins, string, art straws.

What to do
Divide the class into small groups and using the materials suggested, get them to make a simple windmill with sails capable of movement. If any of them have the little toy windmills on sticks (the type you buy at the seaside) they could inspect these for clues. Don't give them too much information; let them experiment for themselves.

You could also ask them to experiment with a lifting bridge model.

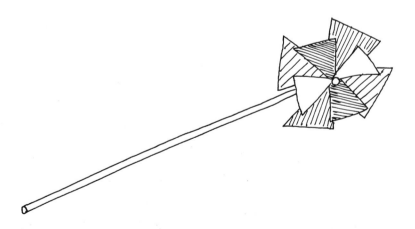

Follow-up
Look at the stories of courage in Holland such as *The Diary of Anne Frank* (Hutchinson Education/Pan) and *The Boy Who Held Back the Sea*, Thomas Locker (Cape), the story of the little boy who stuck his finger in a hole in a dike to save a village.

Look at paintings by Van Gogh and Rembrandt.

Non-fiction books

The term 'literary-based projects', implies fiction. However, the paperback edition of the Oxford English Dictionary defines literature as 'writings that are valued for their beauty of form, especially novels, poetry and plays, etc'. Many non-fiction books come within this category and are to be valued because they are written in the form of an enjoyable story, not just in a textbook style.

I feel the following books come within this category and motivate excellent children's work. They all happen to have an historical flavour, because I enjoy history, but there are equally lovely geography, science, nature and communication books which could lead to successful projects.

The Luttrell Village
Sheila Sancha (Collins)

'In this book I have attempted to put the people of the psalter back into their hills.'
(A psalter is an elaborate prayer book.)

Age range
Eight to eleven.

Synopsis
The Luttrell Village depicts country life in the fourteenth century, by taking you to the very heart of a village and its people. It describes their homes, lives and jobs and the hierarchy within the village. It is more than a textbook because with its maps and the identification of the Lord of the Manor and his wife, it brings the village of Gerneham, now Irnham, to life. Sheila Sancha has based her information on a psalter kept in the British Museum Library. The Psalter was a prayer book commissioned by Sir Geoffrey Luttrell between 1320 and 1340, in which he asked for pictures of himself and his family to be included. The children are able to identify with these characters, and through model-making, drama, writing etc, are able to learn a lot about life of that period.

Setting the scene

Set aside a large area with tables, shelves and other flat areas. The children won't mind having a little less space to work in once they see the display begin to take shape. It is also advisable to have some area of the wall available for display directly beside the flat surfaces.

Display a collection of drawings or models of houses through the ages on a time-line so that they can see what life was like before and after the 1300s. Younger children may still find it hard to appreciate just how long ago the fourteenth century was, but at least an attempt can be made to show the developments in housing and living conditions.

Collect background material on rural medieval life. Nottingham Educational Supplies has an interesting 'Wool Pack'. This can be bought from Nottingham Educational Supplies, Ludlow Hill Road, West Bridgford, Nottingham, NG2 6HD; tel: 0602 - 234251. The Flour Advisory Bureau issues pamphlets on 'The Why and Where of Wheat', and these are available from The Flour Advisory Bureau Ltd, 21 Arlington Street, London SW1A 1RN; tel: 01 - 493 2521.

Make a backdrop

Age range
Eight to eleven.

Group size
Whole class or groups.

What you need
Pictures of medieval halls,
villeins,
forests,
weaving,
deer and old breeds of sheep;
coloured sugar paper,
scissors,
card,
felt-tipped pens,
stapler,
pencils,
paint,
brushes,
adhesive,
large wall space.

What to do
Divide a large wall space in half vertically. On one half display your pictures and facts about sheep, weaving and forestry. On the other half build up a background of different greens, using sugar paper, backing paper or painted paper cut to represent fields. Use two shades of blue to represent the sky. Ask a child to make a large copy of the shield depicted on the front of the book, and the decorative work around it. Mount this on the sky. Make lettering saying 'Luttrell Village' and mount this on the sky as well.

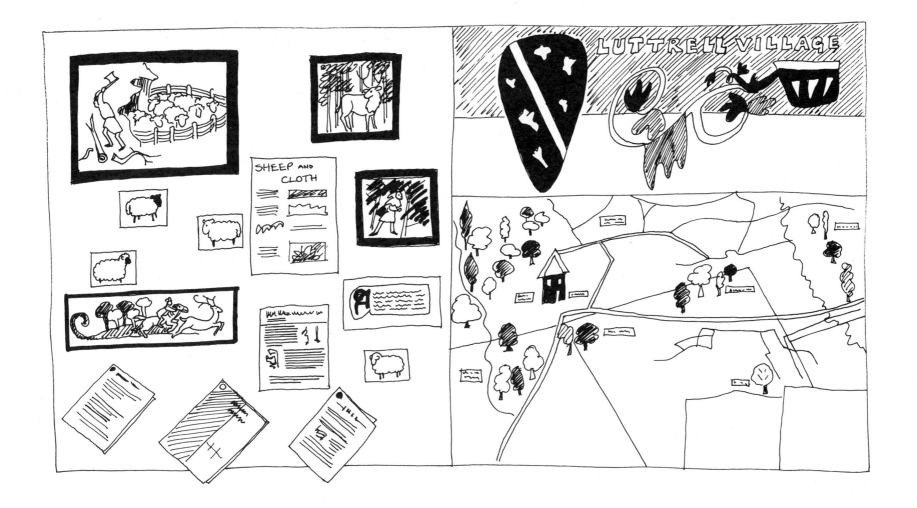

Re-create the map showing Gerneham and the neighbouring villages on the field portion of the frieze. Make labels on white card to correspond with the names in the book. Staple these in the correct position. Use felt-tipped pens to draw in the roads. Give the children small pieces of card. Ask them to draw lots of trees, colour them in and cut them out. Stick cardboard tabs behind each tree and mount them on your display so they stand out from the background. These will represent the timber wood and the wood pasture for the pigs.

If there is a shelf below the wall display, cover it with green paper. Cut hill shapes from card, paint them green and attach them to the bottom of the display to create a three-dimensional effect. Use the remaining shelf area to display models.

Make a village

Age range
Eight to ten.

Group size
Small groups.

What you need
Tables covered in green or brown drapes, cardboard, boxes of various sizes, art straws, paint, brushes. Ask the children to bring in model farm animals, trees and fences.

What to do
Read some of the book and study the map of the village with the class. Look especially at the buildings. Divide the class into small groups and allocate them models to build from cardboard. Three children could make the church, three the windmill and four the demesne and walled garden.

Ask them to colour a cobbled courtyard on white card and stick the buildings on to it. They might like to make a walled entrance. Other children could make crofts or the tents at the fair. A good effect for thatched roofing is to cover card with art straws and paint them yellow to represent straw.

When all your models are finished, create a village setting. The windmill needs to be placed on a hill, so use boxes covered in drapes. Set up the home farm and the church in their correct positions. Scatter the crofts across the landscape. Have a separate area for the fair. Place the children's farm animals around. They will probably bring in plenty, so ask each child to make a list of her belongings. Make model fencing and haystacks to complete the scene. Some things will be out of proportion, but the overall effect will be good.

Medieval drama

Age range
Eight to ten.

Group size
Whole class.

What you need
A large space.

What to do
Continue reading and discussing the book. The children will become familiar with the villagers and their jobs. Over several sessions act out the daily lives of the villagers, and the way their lives vary as the seasons change. The children will readily take on their roles and you can always find a good Lord of the Manor. Crofts and other buildings can be made from tables and stage blocks and the class will soon set about making the village into a real place. A table will become the blacksmith's forge, another the home of Sir Geoffrey's shepherd. A little medieval music will help if you can find some on tape.

Spinning

Age range
Eight to eleven.

Group size
Individuals.

What you need
Fleece or a hank of unspun wool, comb, drop spindle, knitting yarn.

What to do
If you have a whole fleece, let the children examine it; they will soon see where the best of the fleece is to be found. Sort some ready for weaving by picking out any sticks or little pieces of wood, and combing it to align the fibres.

Show the children how to spin using a drop spindle. There are many good books on the subject and the techniques can be mastered with a bit of practice.

Firstly, attach a piece of knitting yarn to the spindle to start you off.

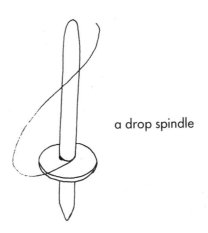

a drop spindle

Divide the end of this yarn into separate threads. Now tease out some of the fleece for spinning. Hold the yarn in your left hand and pull out some fibres from the fleece with your thumb and forefinger. Join these to your yarn so that the fibres mingle. Spin the spindle with your right hand in a clockwise direction. While the spindle is still turning, pull some of the fibres from the fleece in your left hand. As you feel the twist reach your left hand, carry on pulling out the fibres with the right hand and bring the left hand to meet it.

When the spindle reaches the floor, wind the spun yarn on to the spindle and start the process again.

The spinning may be very lumpy and uneven, but it can still be dyed and the texture can be used to make an attractive piece of weaving.

You may only have moderate success with this, but it does at least show the process and the children will enjoy it.

Weaving faces

Age range
Eight to eleven.

Group size
Whole class.

What you need
Looms made from card, sticks or polystyrene tiles, yarns of contrasting colours and thicknesses, scraps of fabric.

What to do
Make a loom from a piece of card with notches cut on opposite edges. Alternatively, you can use four sticks lashed firmly together in a square or a notched polystyrene tile.

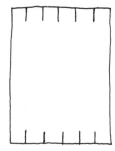

cut notches at both ends of a piece of cardboard

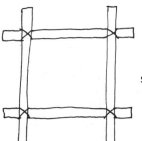

strap four sticks together

Set up the warp threads on your loom, then weave the weft threads, either regularly or in random patterns.

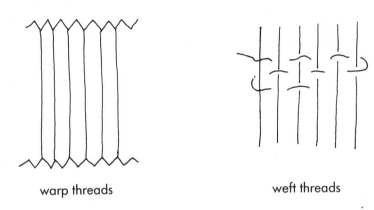

warp threads   weft threads

Polystyrene tiles can be used for making woven faces. Long pieces of yarn can be woven in to represent the hair and shorter pieces can be used for the eyes, nose and mouth. Incorporate pieces of fabric to represent a bow in the hair or a bow tie.

polystyrene tile

weave in yarn for the features and add a fabric bow

Follow-up

There are many other potential activities associated with homes and houses. One possible subject is 'You're never alone at home'. Look at all the small creatures that invade your home and write about them. There are one or two books about the creatures that live in our houses.

Alternatively, create an area entitled 'Be it ever so humble there's no place like home'. Ask the children to bring in old household items that people once used in the home. They will probably bring in objects that you remember from your own childhood. Make a window scene with curtains and set up a table in front of it. Cover the table with a cloth and use it to display the old items.

Go into the area around your school and look at the variety of houses in your neighbourhood. In certain parts of the country you will be lucky enough to have examples of old half-timbered houses. Compare the houses of the children in your class and the range of building materials used. The children can supply drawings of their houses and plans of rooms. This can go into the realms of mathematics, measurement and scale.

Cathedral: The Story of its Construction
David Macaulay (Collins)

'The people of Chutreaux wished to build the longest, widest, highest, and most beautiful cathedral in all of France.'

Age range
Nine to eleven.

Synopsis
David Macaulay tells us the fictional story of a cathedral built in Chutreaux, France. He tells of its conception, of the architects, and the skilled workmen and labourers. He stresses the enormity of the task of the construction which was begun in 1252 and completed in 1338.

A step-by-step guide to its construction is included which indicates the amount of labour and the love that went into such a building. The making of glass and the casting of the bells in medieval times is also shown. This is a good opportunity to bring home to the children the unbelievable determination needed to construct such a building without the aid of modern machinery.

Setting the scene
Make a collection of postcards and pictures of cathedrals. A large display board with tables or stage blocks nearby will be useful. Cover the upper part of the board with a narrow strip of pale blue paper and the rest of the board with pale green paper. On one side of the board put in a blue river cut from paper. Make this tail away into the distance.

Make a forestry area from green paper. Look at the drawings in the book. Cut out some shapes to represent felled trees. Cut out paper ships and stick them on to the river. Cut out white paper sails and staple these on to the masts so that they are raised.

Leave the other half of the board; this will be used later. On the thin strip of blue representing the sky, write the word 'CATHEDRAL' in red letters on a white background. Underneath in black felt-tipped pen write 'The Story of its Construction by David Macaulay'. Add the name of your class.

Try to arrange a visit to a major cathedral after the book has been studied; the children will look at it with a greater understanding and will look out for features that have become familiar to them.

Skilled craftsmen

Age range
Nine to eleven.

Group size
Individuals.

What you need
Drawing paper,
pencils,
writing paper.

What to do
Read about the work of the craftsmen. Show the children the pictures of the craftsmen in the book. Ask them to make large drawings of the craftsmen and to write about their work and their skills. Mount the work ready for display.

Drama skills

Age range
Nine to ten.

Group size
Whole class.

What you need
A large space.

What to do
Get the children to act out the jobs of the master craftsmen. If you can, show them similar tools to the ones that the craftsmen would have used and explain their use. By looking at the tools the children will understand how each was used. They will learn, for example, that the saw the craftsmen used was operated by two people.

Build a cathedral

Age range
Nine to eleven.

Group size
Small groups and individuals.

What you need
Pencils, corrugated card, cardboard tubes, cardboard, scissors, adhesive, art straws, cotton reels, string, small pieces of wood, scrap materials, paper, paint, brushes.

What to do
Using the pictures in the book for reference, draw the outline of a cathedral on the other half of the board that has been left free. The idea is that it will show certain features as though you were looking at a cross-section and not a complete cathedral.

Stick on corrugated card to represent the main outline. Cardboard tubes can be used for pillars. Pieces of card can be cut and bent into shape to form archways and flying buttresses. Use art straws to make rafters and roof trusses. Ask the children to design and make a windlass using cotton reels and string, plus a cardboard handle. A small piece of wood can be loaded on to the end of the string and raised and lowered using the model windlass. The children can construct other machinery from scrap materials. Ask everyone in the class to draw, paint and cut out tiny people and stick them in front of the cathedral. Some children can draw horses and carts and craftsmen at work. Mount the drawings and any written work in the space left around the cathedral.

Finally, cut out a city wall from cardboard, bend and fold it to make towers and cut out a gateway; stick this to the lower half of the display.

Model houses

Age range
Nine to eleven.

Group size
Work in pairs.

What you need
Card, gummed paper, paper, paints, brushes, double-sided sticky tape.

What to do
Ask each pair of children to construct a medieval house from pieces of card. Use gummed paper cut into strips to represent wooden beams and for outlining windows. Paint in the doors and windows. Fold large rectangles of card in half to make roofs for the houses and secure them to the main body of the house with double-sided sticky tape.

Cover the display area with drapes or paper and arrange the houses together in front of the cathedral.

Stained glass windows

Age range
Nine to eleven.

Group size
Small groups.

What you need
Black sugar paper, string, pencils, pins, brightly coloured tissue-paper, adhesive, scissors, white paper.

What to do
Read about how medieval people made glass then ask the children to make their own 'stained glass windows'.

Create as large a rose window as you have space for. Make a large circle on a sheet of black sugar paper by attaching a piece of string to a pencil, then pinning the other end of the string to where you envisage the centre of the circle to be. Hold the string taut and draw the circle.

Cut out the circle and then carefully cut out shapes from within this circle which can be filled in with 'glass' made from tissue-paper.

Instead of trying to put in orderly shapes and large areas of a single colour, create irregular shapes using small scraps of tissue-paper cut in petal and leaf shapes which overlap with each other to make new colours. Leave some areas empty. Windows can be made from other shapes as well. Cut out figures of men from white paper and stick them on the rose window as though they were working on it.

Follow-up

Visit a cathedral, but let the authorities know in advance about your visit so that they can supply you with information and arrange for a guide to talk to the children about the building. Having discussed and read the book, the children will take an interest and be able to ask sensible questions.

Before your visit, re-read the book and look at the plan which is fairly typical of all cathedrals. Discuss its cross-like shape and ask the children why they think it was built like this. Point out that all main entrances are on the west side of the building. The small arm of the cross makes the north and south transept. The main altar is at the east end. Features such as gargoyles can be discussed.

In Search of Tutankhamun
Piero Ventura and Gian Paolo Ceserani (Macdonald)

'In the dark he could see the shapes of all kinds of objects, piled high. The room was glittering with gold.'

Age range
Seven to eleven.

Synopsis
In Search of Tutankhamun is the story of Howard Carter, Lord Carnarvon and his daughter and their wonderful discovery of the treasures and mummified body of King Tutankhamun. There is a good map at the beginning of the book showing Egypt in relation to the Mediterranean Sea. The book also tells of the history of Egypt, the plan for the afterlife, everyday living, hieroglyphics, their buildings, their gods, priests and learning and their wars. The tale of Howard Carter is told quite simply, but the children feel the excitement of the discovery and learn about the detailed work of recording and restoring the finds. They love the details of the sarcophagus and all the coffins which have to be opened in order to find Tutankhamun's body. They are especially fascinated by the story of Howard Carter's mascot, a canary, which is killed by a cobra.

Setting the scene

A large area is needed with display tables. Cut out a large pyramid from card and cover it with sandy coloured paper. Suspend it from the ceiling a little way from a background of sandy colours to create a three-dimensional effect. Set the scene by telling the children about Howard Carter and Lord Carnarvon. Read the chapter 'Valley of the Kings'.

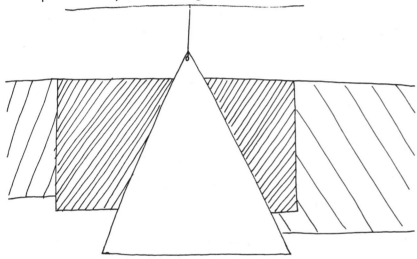

Create a tomb

Age range
Seven to eleven.

Group size
Individuals.

What you need
Pictures of Egyptian art, 19 square grid paper (see photocopiable page 123), pencils, felt-tipped pens, tracing paper, frieze paper, paints, brushes, drapes, card, gold paper.

What to do

Explain to the children how the Egyptians always designed their figures within a set grid framework. For example, the length of a figure from head to toe would take up 19 squares and from foot to knee would take up six squares. The outstretched arms would measure 19 squares from finger tip to finger tip. The figures are depicted so that the shoulders, chest and eyes are seen from the front, and the head, hips and legs are in profile.

The children will need plenty of examples for reference and plenty of practice, but most will cope. After they have drawn their figures on to the grid provided, let them trace the figures and transfer them on to a long frieze which can be used to make the walls of

the tomb. Add Egyptian-style borders, decorations and hieroglyphics. Draw and paint large figures of gods on stiff card and bend these between the walls and the roof of your display area to outline the roof of your tomb. Add some drapes and roll gold coloured paper or card to make some pillars. The overall effect will be very impressive.

Egyptian houses

Age range
Nine to eleven.

Group size
Individuals or small groups.

What you need
Books about ancient Egypt, card, art straws, cardboard tubes, boxes, adhesive, paints, brushes.

What to do
Look at the layout of Egyptian houses ranging from a poor peasant's to a nobleman's house. Point out how the Egyptians liked symmetry in their homes. Look at the materials the Egyptians used for building. This will help the children decide on what colours they will use.

Ask the children to construct model houses using card, art straws, cardboard tubes and boxes. You should soon have a good model Egyptian village. The children might like to bring in model horses and cows; you might even be lucky enough to get a model camel!

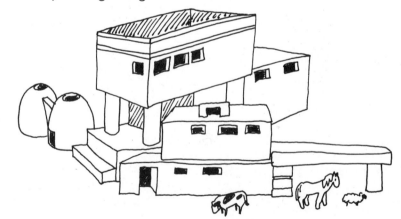

Howard Carter's journal

Age range
Seven to eleven.

Group size
Whole class and individual work.

What you need
Paper,
pencils,
crayons,
felt-tipped pens,
coloured sugar paper.

What to do
Continue reading the book and discuss Howard Carter's discovery and work. Ask the children to write an account of the discovery as though they were writing the journal of Howard Carter, Lord Carnarvon or his daughter, Evelyn. This should produce some very good written work.

Ask each child to make a folder from suitably coloured sugar paper and to insert the written work together with illustrations. The children can then make an interesting cover for the journal.

Make a Pharaoh

Age range
Seven to eleven.

Group size
Individuals or small groups.

What you need
Cardboard, wallpaper, knitting needle, adhesive, string, paint, brushes, clear varnish, white sheeting, threads or knitting yarn, pencils.

What to do
Draw a large outline of a Pharaoh on card. The Pharaoh's head-dress can be one of several different shapes, which you can copy from books, but this one is the simplest.

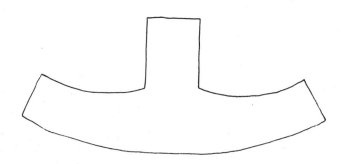

Ask the children to make large cardboard bracelets and anklets. Let each child make a bead to make up a necklace. Cut out an elongated triangle from wallpaper for each bead. The size of the triangle will determine the size of the bead; the longer the triangle, the more rounded the beads will be.

Starting from the broad end of the triangle, roll the paper up with the pattern on the outside. Secure the point of the triangle in place with a spot of adhesive to form the bead.

Vary the size of the beads so that you have large ones in the middle of the necklace and small ones around the back. Coat them with clear varnish.

Thread them on to a length of string. Make several strands and put them around the Pharaoh's neck. Tie a piece of white sheeting around the Pharaoh's waist together with some colourful cords.

Make a twisted cord by cutting several threads or pieces of yarn three times the required length of cord. Knot the strands together at the ends to make a loop. Ask a child to hold tightly on to one end and a second child to insert a pencil into the other end. Hold the strands taut then ask the second child to turn the pencil

to twist the cord. Put the two ends of the twisted cord together and it will twist back on itself. Secure the ends of the cord with knots.

Mummies

Age range
Seven to ten.

Group size
Individuals.

What you need
Dolls, clear food wrapping, old sheets torn into bandages, plaster of Paris, paint, brushes, cardboard, gold powder paint.

What to do
Wrap the dolls carefully in clear food wrapping to protect them, then wrap them from head to toe in old sheets torn into bandages. Cover the bandaged form with a thick layer of plaster of Paris.

When the plaster is completely dry, paint the mummy using gold powder paint, then add decorations in bright colours. Make a sarcophagus from cardboard.

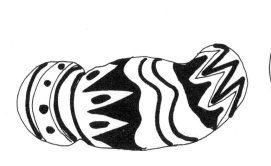

Follow-up

This project provides plenty of scope for maths work, such as learning the Egyptian number system – (see *Bright Ideas History*).

The Egyptians' use of symmetry in the design of their buildings can also be incorporated into maths and PE.

Talk to the children about the pyramids. This can lead on to looking at angles. Show the children how the angles in a circle add up to 360° by drawing a cross in a circle.

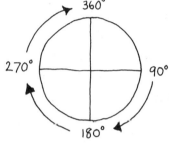

Then demonstrate how the angles on a straight line are equal to 180°. This can be done by cutting the corners off any triangle and then fitting these on to a straight line. Work can be done on triangles that have different names and properties. Mobiles can be made from a simple net and made to look like pyramids. Colour these and suspend them from the ceiling.

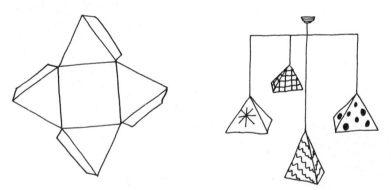

Dinosaurs – a Lost World in Three Dimensions
Keith Moseley (Methuen)

'This book shows how some of those ancient animals lived and died in a world no longer with us.'

Age range

Seven to eleven. Infants love this subject and some of the activities could be used with five- to seven-year-olds.

Synopsis

This is a colourful book which gives clear and simple facts about dinosaurs, together with a good introduction. It describes a number of different dinosaurs giving their measurements and weight; this, unfortunately, is not in metric so some conversion will have to be done.

The *Brachiosaurus* is compared with an elephant, giraffe, rhinoceros and hippopotamus which helps children to understand just how large some dinosaurs were. There is a lovely demonstration of the *Ankylosaurus* – by pulling a tab the club-like tail moves into operation. The book ends with a discussion as to why dinosaurs died out.

Setting the scene

Set the scene by making a background frieze. Use deep greens and sandy colours to create a swampy background.

To create a three-dimensional effect, make trees by rolling up newspapers, secure them with sticky tape then cover them with green crêpe paper cut to one and a half times the length of the roll of newspaper. Cut the excess crêpe paper to represent fronds of foliage.

Add volcanoes cut from card. Lava can be made from red and yellow tissue and crêpe paper. Cut fern shapes from wallpaper.

Add a time line so that the children have some idea of how long ago dinosaurs lived, although it will be difficult for them to imagine. A collection of fossils would be useful.

Studying size

Age range
Seven to nine.

Group size
Whole class.

What you need
Chalk, metre sticks or trundle wheels.

What to do
Read the book, its three-dimensional nature gives instant motivation. Look at the size of the *Brachiosaurus*. It weighs as much as twelve large elephants. Go out on the playground and measure out the length of its neck. Look at the size of other dinosaurs and measure them out on the playground.

Collage

Age range
Seven to ten.

Group size
Whole class.

What you need
Paper,
adhesive,
fabric,
tissue-paper,
cardboard egg boxes,
paints,
brushes.

What to do
Choose some of the smaller dinosaurs for a life-sized collage in the classroom. Draw their outlines on frieze paper. Ask the children to fill in the shapes with collage materials. Encourage the use of bright colours, rather than just muddy greens and browns. Cut out and mount the dinosaurs on your background frieze and on other wall spaces. Add their names. If you have a height card against which the children measure themselves, put it at the side of the dinosaurs. The children can then compare their own size against the dinosaurs. A graph could be made to compare the sizes of different dinosaurs.

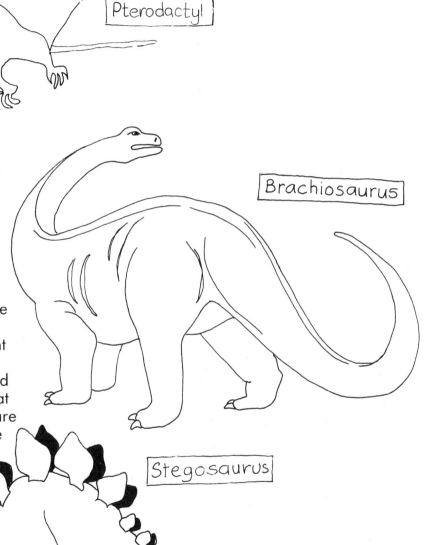

Pterodactyl

Brachiosaurus

Stegosaurus

Dinosaur poems 1

Age range
Seven to eleven.

Group size
Whole class.

What you need
The Tail of the Trinosaur, Charles Causley (Brockhampton/Hamlyn), paper, crayons, a background space.

What to do
Read *The Tail of the Trinosaur* which is told in 24 'shakes'. The children will want to repeat some of it. Concentrate on the procession in the market square and all of the guests: the Mayor, Mayoress, brownies, guides, Sammy Smother and his mother.

   Ask the children to draw the characters and colour them. Cut them out and put them on a suitable background. Make a large picture of the Trinosaur, and put cardboard tabs on to the back so that it can be raised from the background. Write out a little of the letter by 'Signs himself A Friend'. All sorts of details can be added about Dunborough Town. Little sections of the poem can be written out and mounted.

Dinosaur poems 2

Age range
Seven to eleven.

Group size
Whole class and individual work.

What you need
Oh Dinosaur and Other Poems, Barbara Ireson (Corgi – out of print but try libraries), paper, pencils, felt-tipped pens.

What to do
Read Barbara Ireson's dinosaur poems. The illustrations are very amusing. Then ask the children to write their own poems or word pictures about one particular dinosaur. When finished, the poems can be written out and suitably illustrated. They might like to draw the dinosaur first and put the poem inside the shape.

Tyrannosaurus Rex was the
biggest of them all.
He was very big
He was six metres tall.
He weighed seven tons and that is heavy
And when he'd had his dinner,
he had a fat belly.
He had got teeth 20 centimetres long
They were very sharp and very very strong.
They went through things quick as a flash,
He ate all kinds of things including trash,
He used his great legs for getting up speed
And sometimes he used to eat up
    some weeds.
He galloped fast along the land.
And made giant footprints in
    the sand.

Poetry

Poetry is at times sadly neglected in primary schools. Not at first, perhaps, when nursery and reception classes read and chant nursery and finger rhymes together. As the children grow older, teachers choose modern poets such as Roger McGough, who produces lots of very humorous, witty anthologies, which have a place and value in promoting poetry with children. But there is much more to poetry than just this. In *This Way Delight* (Faber), Herbert Read says of poetry, 'You must not even think of it as "literature" which is an ugly word invented by schoolmasters'. He goes on to talk of magic and mystery in poetry: this is the very essence of why we should not neglect it.

Poetry should not be undervalued within the classroom. Some teachers are concerned that children might try to use rhyme and rhythm in their own poetry, but this shouldn't be a worry. What we need to convey is that in poetry every word counts and that, unlike a story, you haven't got all day to come to the point. In poetry you are making pictures or expressing your feelings by making language come alive. There doesn't need to be a great set of rules.

The following poems will fire children's enthusiasm and motivate them to write the most wonderful poetry and word pictures.

Please Mrs Butler
Allan Ahlberg (Kestrel/Puffin)

'Scissors don't lose themselves,
Melt away or explode.'

Age range
Eight to eleven.

Group size
Whole class and individual work.

What you need
Paper, pencils, paints, brushes, scissors.

What to do
This is a good book to use at the beginning of the school year when projects such as 'Ourselves' or 'Our class' might be looked at, so reserve some display space for it. Start with the children drawing and painting pictures of themselves.

Cut out the work and display it grouped together. You could entitle it 'Our class: What a crowd!' if your visitors and parents have a sense of humour.

Read a selection of the poems to the class, then suggest titles for the children's own poems or word pictures such as:
'School dinners'
'When Mr . . . or Mrs . . . is angry'
'When I am naughty'
'A good piece of work'
'School service'
'A visit from the headteacher'
'Excuses'.
These examples all work very well and poetry can often be used to develop good prose. Compile all the poems to form a class book.

This Way Delight
poems selected by Herbert Read (Faber)

'All in green went my love riding
on a great horse of gold
into the silver dawn.'

Age range
Seven to eleven.

Group size
Whole class and individual work.

What you need
Pencils, paper, paints, brushes.

What to do
Read some of the poems to the children. 'Old Cat Care' by Richard Hughes, 'Milk for the Cat' by Harold Monro, 'All in green went my love riding' by e e cummings and 'Overheard on a Saltmarsh' by Harold Monro, are particularly good. Let each child choose a poem about

colour, then get them to draw or paint a picture to illustrate it. Mount and display the pictures with quotations from the poems.

When the children have experienced a wealth of colour poetry, they will be ready to write down and illustrate some of their own images. Discuss the different ways of illustrating a poem: around or below the poem, or writing a poem over a complete page of illustration. Mount the class work into a book and ask one of the children to design a cover.

The Quangle Wangle's Hat
Edward Lear, pictures by Helen Oxenbury (Heinemann/Puffin)

'The Frog and the Fimble Fowl
(The Fimble Fowl with a corkscrew leg);'

Age range
Seven to eleven.

Group size
Whole class.

What you need
Pencils, paper, crayons.

What to do
This is a nonsense poem very much in line with many of Lear's poems, full of humour, about the Quangle Wangle's Hat, a hundred and two feet wide, and all the imaginary creatures who come to live in it.

Read the poem, but don't let the children see the illustrations yet. Then either allocate children creatures to draw from the poem or let them choose for themselves. See what amazing illustrations they come up with.

Edward Lear's imaginary creatures create wonderful images such as the luminous nose, Crumpetty Tree, Olympian Bear, Blue Baboon and Bisky Bat.

Encourage the children to invent their own imaginary creatures, name them and describe their unusual actions or their travels on unusual journeys. They can then illustrate them.

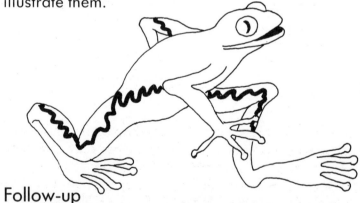

Follow-up
Read Edward Lear's *The Owl and the Pussy Cat* (Piccolo). This poem is good because of the repetitive chorus which the children will enjoy chanting.

The Lady of Shalott
Alfred, Lord Tennyson

'"The curse is come upon me!" cried
The Lady of Shalott.'

Age range
Nine to eleven.

Group size
Individuals.

What you need
Materials for display work: paper, pencils, paints, brushes.
Materials for dolls: dolly pegs, felt-tipped pens, pipe-cleaners, pink tissue-paper, fabric scraps, card, adhesive, needle and thread.

What to do
This is the magical tale of the doomed Lady of Shalott: a sad tale, but one with beautiful images created by skilled writing. It is by no means an easy poem due to its language because the poem was written in 1852, but with careful explanations the children will become enchanted with the story.

Read the first part of the poem. There is a lot to discuss here such as what can be seen on either side of the river, the beauty of the aspens, many-towered

Camelot, barges drawn by horses and the reapers in the moonlight listening to the whispers. Ask the children to interpret these images in drawings and paintings. Ask some of the children to paint a background frieze for the work.

Read the second part of the poem. Ask the children what they think it would be like to weave by night and day watching the world go by through a mirror, knowing that if they turn to look at the real world a curse will come upon them. Ask the children to create more of the scene showing the Lady of Shalott spinning. You might incorporate spinning and weaving (see *The Luttrell Village* section on pages 73 and 74).

Get the children to write the story in their own words. The work can then be mounted on the large wall frieze.

Read part three in the same way. It is not often that children are presented with anything with a sad ending, but you can discuss with them that the fate of the Lady of Shalott was perhaps preferable to being imprisoned and to living an unreal life and not being able to join in the activities that she could see in her mirror.

Follow-up

This would link in nicely with work on legends such as King Arthur and the Knights of the Round Table. You could play some music from the sound-track of *Camelot* (Warner Brothers) (your local library might help you here). The song about the weather sums up the magic of Camelot.

Do some work on costumes by dressing peg dolls in medieval costumes. Use felt-tipped pens to draw a face on the head of a dolly peg, then wrap pipe-cleaners around it for arms. Cover the pipe-cleaners in pink tissue-paper cut into small strips. Use scraps of fabric and card stuck or stitched into place to make a dress, a pointed hat and a veil. Make other peg dolls in male costume.

Hiawatha
Henry Wadsworth Longfellow

'Ewa-yea! my little owlet!
Who is this that lights the wigwam?'

Age range
Seven to eleven.

Group size
Individuals.

What you need
Drums and any other types of percussion instruments, paper, pencils, crayons.

What to do
Hiawatha is a very long narrative poem about the birth of an Indian boy, his childhood, adolescence, courtship, marriage and his life as a warrior. It is based on the true story of an Indian leader and hero. It is written in such a way that you can choose small sections to read which will stand on their own. The remarkable thing is the rhythm, which, like Ravel's *Bolero*, keeps to the same beat the whole way through.

Read some of the poem. Clap out the rhythm. Does the rhythm remind the children of anything? What musical instrument does it remind them of? They may come to the conclusion that it sounds like drums. Ask them to beat out the rhythm using drums, beaters and other percussion instruments.

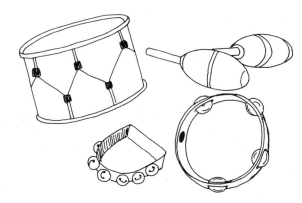

Choose one of the sections such as the passage about Nokomis' teaching which draws forth beautiful images. Ask the children to draw and colour their interpretations of some of these images. Could they describe their own surroundings to a little child using poetical phrases? Perhaps they could give new names to everything around them, making the classroom seem magical by bringing objects to life. These activities are successful with older children.

Follow-up
This could be part of a project on Indians. The colour, the descriptions of the way of life and the images inspire children and motivate them into becoming good writers and artists.

Listen to a recording of *Hiawatha's Wedding Feast* by Samuel Coleridge-Taylor. Your local library might be able to find this for you.

Peacock Pie
Walter de la Mare (Faber)

'Slowly, silently, now the moon
Walks the night in her silver shoon;'

Age range
Seven to eleven.

Group size
Whole class.

What you need
Pencils, paper.

What to do
This anthology of poems introduces all the poetic devices. These will inspire children to produce better written work. However, although it is important to develop writing styles, pure enjoyment of listening should not be forgotten.

Choose some of the poems which are interesting to listen to. Ask the children to pick out their favourite words and the best descriptions.

The following poems are good examples:
'Some One' (They will enjoy learning this one off by heart.)
'The Ship of Rio'
'Hide and Seek'
'Full Moon'
'Sooeep!'
'Sam'
'Nicholas Nye'
'Five Eyes'
'The Ride-by-Nights'
'Nobody Knows'.

Read 'Five Eyes'. You cannot read 'Five Eyes' any other way than rhythmically, stressing the wonderful rhyme, alliteration and movement. Ask the children why it is called 'Five Eyes'.

Get them to write a word picture about cats describing the way they move. The cats could be in a house, a garden or a field.

Read 'The Ride-by-Nights'. This is a good poem to read at Hallowe'en. Not many children will understand what 'Charlie's Wain' or 'Dragons Feet' are, so mention the Milky Way as a clue.

These poems are good for encouraging the development of different sorts of writing and for appreciating rhythm.

Read 'Some One'. Look for alliteration and the way sounds are described, eg tap-tapping, the screech of the owl's call, whistling and knocking. Ask the children to write a word picture which conjures up night-time. Look at the repetition of 'At all, at all, at all'.

Read 'Silver'. Here is an opportunity to show children how inanimate objects can become like real people. In this case it is the moon casting her silver shadows over the garden and house. Here the letter 'S' is repeated to beautiful effect.

'Witch Goes Shopping'
Lilian Moore from Witch Poems ed Daisy Wallace (Bell & Hyman)

'"This," says Witch, now all a-twitch
"Is a crazy store."'

Age range
Five to eleven.

Group size
Individuals.

What you need
Poems and stories about witches (older children might like to look at Shakespeare's *Macbeth*), paper, pencils.

What to do
This is a poem about a witch who makes a shopping list of things such as 'six bats' wings', 'slugs and bugs', then takes herself off upon her broomstick to the local supermarket, whereupon she cannot find any of the ingredients on the shelves.

To set the scene you need to set aside a small area to display writing and illustrations. A quick method of setting up a witch or magic display is to use yellow backing paper and to cut out black silhouettes and black lettering. Make a border out of trees, eyes, castles, etc.

Read the poem 'Witch Goes Shopping'. This will lead naturally on to a discussion about spells. From this you can suggest as a title 'Spell to make . . .'. The children can provide the rest of the title. Give them the first line 'Into the pot there must go . . .'.

This poem was written by an eight-year-old:

> Spell to make city into jungle
>
> Into the pot there must go
> Toad's blood
> Snail's slime
> Swamp's mud
> Bat's teeth – 29
> Snake's scale
> Human's nail
> Spider's legs
> That look like pegs.
> Lightening, lightening, strike the pot,
> So my spell is nice and hot.

Follow-up
This can form the basis of a topic about magic or work for Hallowe'en. Traditional activities can be incorporated such as making masks or apple bobbing. Make a spell and set it to music. Ask the children to act out making a spell.

'The Hairy Toe'

Traditional American in Hist Whist, collected by Dennis Saunders (Pan)

'"Where's my Hair-r-ry To-o-oe?
Who's got my Hair-r-ry To-o-oe?"'

Age range
Eight to eleven.

Group size
Whole class and individual work.

What you need
Space for drama, tape recorder, pencils, paper, crayons.

What to do
This is a nonsensical poem, full of awe, about a woman who finds a hairy toe and its owner who comes looking for it. Read the poem, making sure that you make the voice of the owner of the hairy toe suitably terrifying.

Ask the children to act out the poem. You need a child to act the part of the woman and one to act the owner of the hairy toe. A group of children can become the wind which growls like an animal. Others can form the shape of the house which creaks and groans. This will make an effective 'sound picture'. Ask the whole class to tell the poem through sounds only: creaks for the house, cracks for the door, groans and moans. I suspect that it would end in a loud scream. Tape this, then play it back to the children.

Ask the children to make their own poem using the same structure but with different objects that they have found beginning with 'Give me back my . . .'. Ask the children to write these out and illustrate them suitably. The work can then be displayed or made into a class book.

'Welsh Incident',
Robert Graves in The New Golden Treasury of English Verse (Macmillan)

'But that was nothing to what things came out
From the sea caves of Criccieth yonder.'

Age range
Eight to eleven.

Group size
Individuals.

What you need
Paper, pencils, crayons, material to make a book with a suitable binder.

What to do
This is a narrative poem, written in such a way as to imitate the Welsh intonation. This is important for it helps to extend the children's knowledge of what a poem can be. The poem has a sing-song rhythm – use this to demonstrate to children how words can be used to create effect. It is a poem of mystery and humour, it gives lots of description and hints, and it sets up a wonderful scene on the beach. However, the reader never actually finds out what the creatures mentioned are and the poem ends in mid-story.

Read the poem several times to the class and discuss it, as not everything will be immediately apparent to the children. Give each child two or three different lines of the poem, then ask them to write out and illustrate the lines on a sheet of paper. Assemble these in order and ask one of the children to make a suitable cover. The 'Welsh Incident' then comes to life and the children's interpretations of the creatures are truly wonderful. The arrangement of the classroom depends on how far you wish to take the work. You might wish to relate this to a topic on holidays.

Follow-up
The poem ends 'What did the Mayor do?' 'I was coming to that'. Ask the children to write what they think the Mayor did next.

Books for stimulus

Primary schools are usually filled with large display boards which can be a mixed blessing. Some teachers revel in displaying children's work and, like myself, use this as a way of unwinding after a hard day! More seriously, display can be used as a means of motivating children and giving their work an extra dimension.

Illustrations from books are a lovely means with which you can cover large display areas in halls or libraries or use to make your classroom extra-special at Christmas.

To this end, Raymond Briggs' *Father Christmas* and *The Snowman* (Picture Puffins) provide wonderful stimulus. Choose some of the best illustrations in these books and bring them to life. The front cover of *Father Christmas* makes a beautiful Christmas display if it is drawn very large.

Father Christmas
Raymond Briggs (Picture Puffin)

Age range
Five to eight.

Group size
Whole class.

What you need
Paper, pencils, cotton wool, red and gold foil, black sugar paper, scissors, adhesive, paints, brushes, scraps of fabric, artificial snow.

What to do
Draw a large outline of Father Christmas as shown on the cover of the book. Let the children fill in the jacket, hat and gloves with small pieces of red foil in the style of a mosaic. Fill the beard with cotton wool and add a cotton wool trim to his hat and gloves. Cut out a large foil buckle. Paint in a rosy face and fill in the sack, bag and flask with paint or scraps of fabric. Display him by drawing and cutting out lettering as it is on the front cover. Use artificial snow on your chosen background.

Many of the other pictures can be imitated in collage. The pictures of the houses with lights on and people in bed and Father Christmas on the roof is beautiful when made into a collage using glitter and gold foil. The older children will take great care with this and add details such as holly wreaths on the doors and Christmas trees at the windows. Father Christmas eating his sandwiches by a chimney pot is another good example. At Christmas the use of foil, glitter, gold paint etc, is essential if you want to make the displays stand out.

The Snowman
Raymond Briggs (Picture Puffin)

Age range
Five to eight.

Group size
Whole class.

What you need
Frieze paper, coloured paper, scissors, adhesive, paint, brushes, glitter, cotton wool.

What to do
This book is ideal for making a huge frieze for the classroom. Choose some key pictures from the book such as the little boy standing back looking at the Snowman, the Snowman and the boy flying or the Snowman and the boy landing.

For the first two scenes mount on to frieze paper pine trees cut from paper in various shades of green, or paint on green and silver trees.

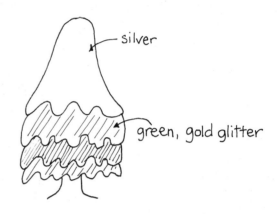

Include bare winter trees with clumps of gold glitter added. Give everyone something to do by asking the class to paint children in winter clothing, cut them out and stick them on to the snow.

For the picture of the Snowman landing, cut out plenty of large snowflakes from white paper, using a variety of patterns, and stick them around him. Use cotton wool for the Snowman. Make sure that the little boy's dressing gown is the same in both of the flying pictures.

$2 \times 1 = 2$

$2 \times 5 = 10$

$2 \times 4 = 8$

$2 \times 3 = 6$

Introduce other snowmen, graduating in size from large to small. Build up a pattern of holly berries on their hats, put stripes on their scarves and buttons on their bodies to correspond with the two times table.

Classic Fairy Tales
Hans Christian Andersen (Gollancz)

Age range
Five to nine.

Group size
Whole class.

What you need
Frieze paper, blue and silver foil, white paper, tissue-paper, gummed paper, cotton wool, silver glitter, blue and silver paint, pale blue paper.

What to do
Snow is such a lovely theme at Christmas time and displays can be left up well into the New Year. Hans Andersen's fairy tales can provide inspiration for lovely displays.

Look at the pictures in 'The Snowman', 'The Snow Queen' and 'The Little Match Girl'. The main pictures from each of these stories look most effective if displayed together on three panels. Make a border for each panel in silver foil cut with a decorative edge.

Draw outlines of the figures on to frieze paper and ask the children to fill them with collage materials. Use blue and white for a wintery effect. Encourage the use of as many different materials as possible. Be generous with glitter and foil; it really is worth it.

Nicola Bayley's Book of Nursery Rhymes
(Puffin)

Age range
Eight to eleven.

Group size
Individuals.

What you need
Pencils, paper, squares of hessian, scissors, pins, fabric scraps, needles, threads, adhesive, buttons, sequins, trimmings.

What to do
Look through the pictures in the book with the children. Look at the colours and suggest some ways in which they could translate them into materials and stitches. Ask the children to choose a nursery rhyme (it doesn't have

to be one in this book) and ask them to translate it into a design for a wall-hanging. I can recommend 'Mary, Mary', 'The Old Woman who Lived in a Shoe', 'The Crooked Man', 'Miss Muffet' or 'The Cat and the Fiddle'.

Give each child a good sized piece of hessian. Older children will be capable of sewing the frayed edges down themselves, but you might have to iron and stick down the edges for younger children. While hessian

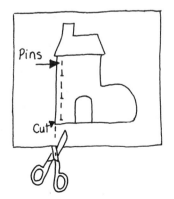

gives a good background, it is not always the easiest material to sew on.

Ask the children first to draw their designs on paper, then cut them up to make paper patterns.

Next ask them to choose the most appropriate types of fabric to bring their pictures to life, pin on the paper patterns and cut out the shapes.

Sew or stick the fabric pieces on to the hessian. Encourage the children to decorate the pictures with buttons, sequins, trimmings and simple embroidery stitches, though some might want to try out some fancy stitches.

The wall-hangings can then be displayed by slotting the hessian into plastic book binders and threading cord through to hang it.

Other good books which are useful for stimulus both for display and fabric ideas are:
Jim and the Beanstalk, Raymond Briggs (Picture Puffin)
Tale of Peter Rabbit, Beatrix Potter (Warne)
Moses The Kitten, James Herriot (Michael Joseph/ Piccolo)
The Ghost Downstairs, Leon Garfield (Kestrel/Puffin)
Danny, the Champion of the World, Roald Dahl (Cape/ Puffin).

Organising a Literature Week

Many schools organise book weeks where the main emphasis of the week is upon books, story telling, visiting authors, book fairs and writing. A lot of schools organise this event to coincide with the National Book Week, in which case I would advise booking authors well in advance. Local libraries sort out their programmes very early and you may wish to enlist their help during this week. Whenever a week is fixed it is vital that the organiser starts to plan six months before the event in order to ensure that it runs smoothly.

Planning ahead

At my school, we organised a book week where every day events took place which were designed to promote the love of books and creative writing. However, the work was not all slotted into one week. In September a meeting was held amongst the nursery, infant and junior staff, to agree upon a programme beginning in January and culminating in a Literature Week in March. Because of my enthusiasm for literature-based projects, I wanted to find an author who had written books which could be used across the full age range – a tall order when you are dealing with four-to eleven-year-olds. However, I knew that Helen Cresswell, a local author, had written books for this age range and I put it to the staff that perhaps each class or year could choose a particular title of hers and try out a literature-based project. I offered them the sort of guide-lines that are in the introduction of this book and suggested that a visit by Helen Cresswell in Literature Week should be the finale to the children's work. I arranged with Helen Cresswell that she would visit the school on two afternoons, once

to work with the nursery and infants and finally to talk to the juniors.

I also asked a local bookseller to supply a set of Helen Cresswell titles on a sale or return basis – an unnecessary worry as we sold all but two books and took dozens of orders. The children could then have copies signed by Helen on her last visit. She took away a supply of gummed labels to sign which she returned promptly and these were stuck inside the books which had been ordered as soon as they were supplied.

The next job was to ask County Library if they could supply me with as many of Helen Cresswell's books as possible including those titles which were out of print. This was one of the earliest tasks to be done because often staff like to plan a long way in advance and know exactly what they are going to be doing the following year.

Using ideas

Planning ahead allows time for other ideas to come to you. I knew of another school whose teachers and children dressed as book characters for a day. What a lovely idea! At first some staff were a little reticent but an 'I'll dress up' from the headteacher spurred everyone on. They had to send letters out well in advance to warn parents and then to send out several reminders. I

decided to link my own literature-based project with a dance/drama which my class could show the school on the final day of Literature Week. We did two performances, one for the infant and nursery classes, and one for the juniors. Our final ending to the week was a 'Literature Trail' where at an appointed time we moved around the whole of the school, clockwise, so that the children and staff could look at all the project work which had been done. We are a large school with a split site, but this still worked well, some children going into rooms and book corners which they hadn't seen for a long time, so this created quite a lot of excitement.

Reasons for success

As organiser of such an event I was delighted by the whole thing. It worked well for the following reasons:

● My enthusiasm convinced the staff that they would enjoy a literature-based project. Some teachers took up to three months in preparation, but others spent less time. The teacher in charge of mathematics confessed to not having taught maths for two weeks in the final run up to Literature Week.

● The programme of events was planned well in advance and several staff meetings were held to iron out any problems.

● The senior staff fully supported the event and gave helpful suggestions.

● The parents were wonderful when it came to dressing-up day.

● We had chosen an author who could not only offer us the right level of books but could come and work with the children at their own level.

● The County Library staff became involved and showed us films and told stories.

● An inspector was willing to come into school and share our week.

● The staff worked very hard in displaying their children's work and were totally committed to the idea.

Looking at the week

Certain things came to light: I had invited authors to talk to the children before, but not always when the children had been familiar with their writing. A bonus for us was that *Moondial* by Helen Cresswell (Faber/Puffin), was on BBC Television for the six weeks leading up to our event. So when Helen Cresswell came to visit the school, the children felt that they already knew her. They were excited to meet someone whose writing had been the focal point for their work for several weeks and they were able to think of some very interesting questions.

At break time we managed to get all the children on to the yard; nursery, infants and juniors. The atmosphere was electric. No-one misbehaved, each child was too interested in looking at the others. The headteacher arranged for two parties, one for the infant and nursery classes, and one for the juniors. This was done in such a way that each class had room to parade in front of all the others and the children had to guess the characters.

On reflection I could have done with more copies of Helen Cresswell's books to sell. I was given 13 titles, four copies of each. I kept one copy of each for display and used the others to sell to the children. I reflected upon whether the whole event had been too much effort, or whether it paid enough dividends to be worthwhile. The answer most certainly was 'yes' to the latter.

I can thoroughly recommend dressing-up. The atmosphere as the children walked to school and through the gate was wonderful. Hundreds of mums with cameras appeared – even binoculars! As for the staff, dressing-up really got us to let our hair down. The infant staff represented St Trinians. The headteacher was Mr Plod and I was Noddy. We had characters ranging from Fagin to the Mad Hatter; Pinnochio to Superman. We had one of the 101 Dalmatians who cocked 'her' leg up when 'she' passed a tub of daffodils placed in the entrance hall. Even the school secretary entered into the spirit of things as Miss Muffet, typing all day with a large rubber spider sitting upon her shoulder.

Positive results

The Literature Week seemed to motivate all the children in my class. I chose Helen Cresswell's *Ellie and the Hagwitch* (Patrick Hardy/Corgi) to use with my second year junior class and I cannot think of any child who was not motivated to work well and to think in an original way. It promoted excellent writing of a quality I did not think possible with second years. I did notice on my walk around the Literature Trail that excellent writing had been done throughout the school. It seemed to introduce humour into the children's writing and it made children want to read other books by Helen Cresswell. Some strove to read titles which were a little too hard for them but they were willing to have a go. It produced excellent art and craft work. I saw another teacher's interpretation of *The Night-watchmen*. He, with his children had constructed an enormous workmen's hut and had put inside it all the things that are listed in the story.

It produced a lot of good language and discussion work; it helped children to work together and it helped the staff to work together as a team and we broke down the divisions of nursery, infant and junior.

It was a good public relations exercise and it was reported by the local press. Most of all it achieved its aim. It promoted the love of books and reading and the use of good language.

Reproducible material

Communications, see page 22

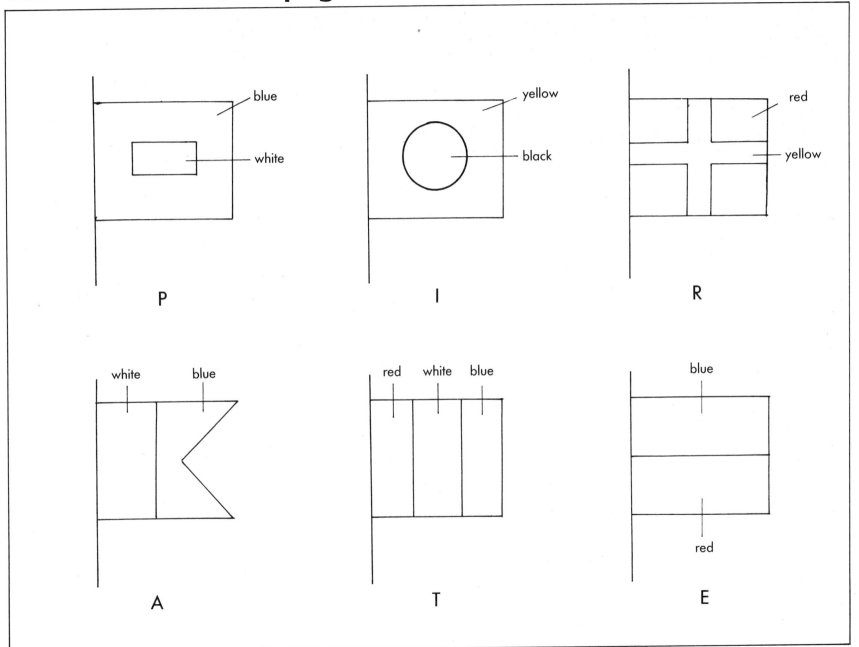

Communications, see page 22

Morse code		M − −	T −
A • −	G − − •	N − •	U • • −
B − • • •	H • • • •	O − − −	V • • • −
C − • − •	I • •	P • − − •	W • − −
D − • •	J • − − −	Q − − • −	X − • • −
E •	K − • −	R • − •	Y − • − −
F • • − •	L • − • •	S • • •	Z − − • •

You are what you eat, see page 32

NAME _____

Remember to fill in this chart daily.

	Monday	Tuesday	Wednesday	Thursday	Friday	Saturday	Sunday	
Dairy products: cheese, milk, eggs								
Fruit Vegetables Salads								
Meat Fish								
Pulses: peas, beans Pasta Nuts								
Junk foods: fast food, chips, crisps								
Drinks (How many?)								

Go through every meal, including snacks between meals and mark the boxes with ticks, eg if you eat an apple, lettuce, tomato and cabbage on Monday your box will have four ticks.

Study of water birds, see page 37

Use this chart each time you look up information. Write the information in the space provided

Name of bird Habitat ie where does it live? Size of bird	
Colour of plumage – feathers Do they change colour at all? When? Description of bird	
Call of the bird Colour of eggs Does it live in more than one country?	

Draw a picture of the bird or its eggs and colour carefully		Enter any other information here Write down the author and title of the books you have used

Soft toy, see page 37

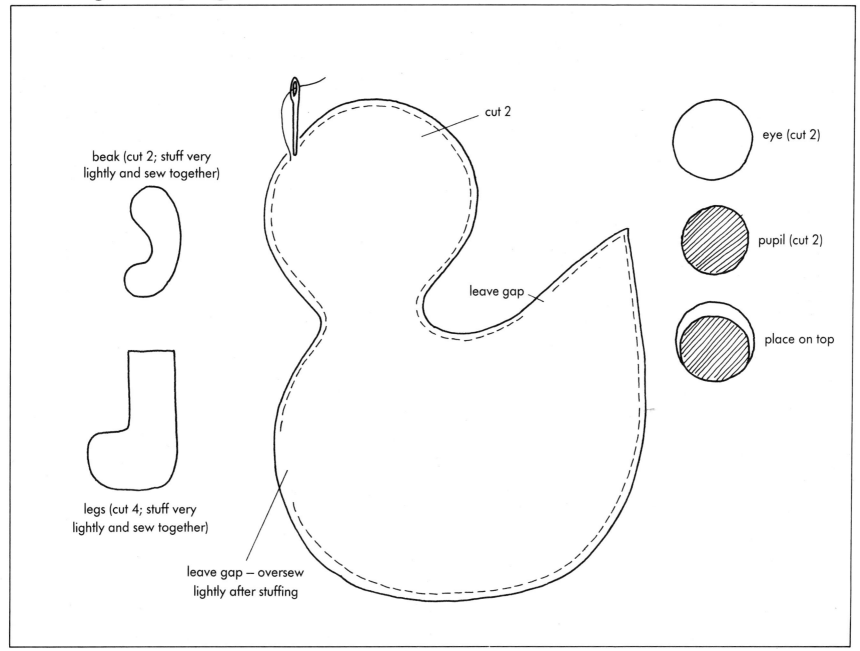

cut 2

beak (cut 2; stuff very lightly and sew together)

leave gap

legs (cut 4; stuff very lightly and sew together)

leave gap — oversew lightly after stuffing

eye (cut 2)

pupil (cut 2)

place on top

Snake shapes and poems, see page 52

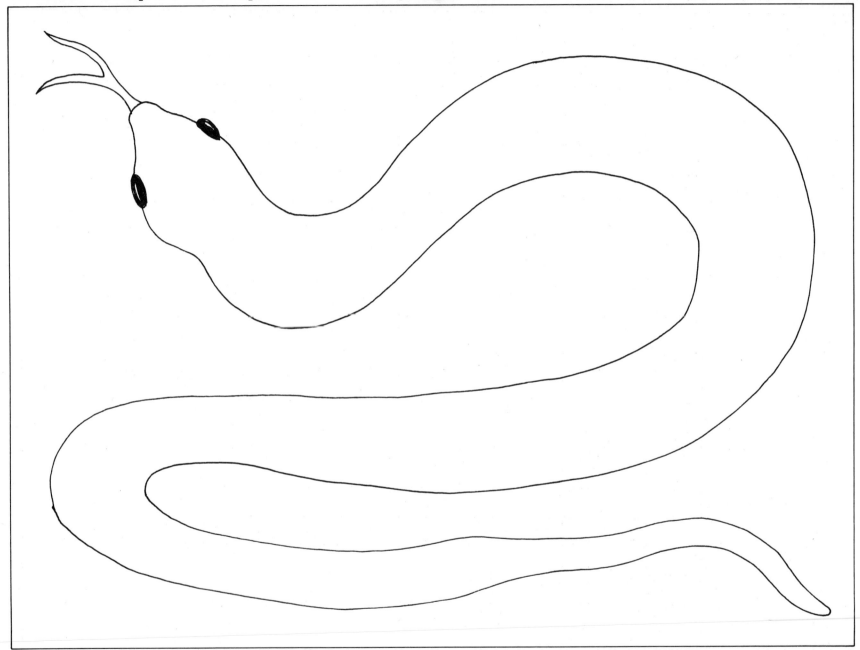

Create a tomb, see page 81

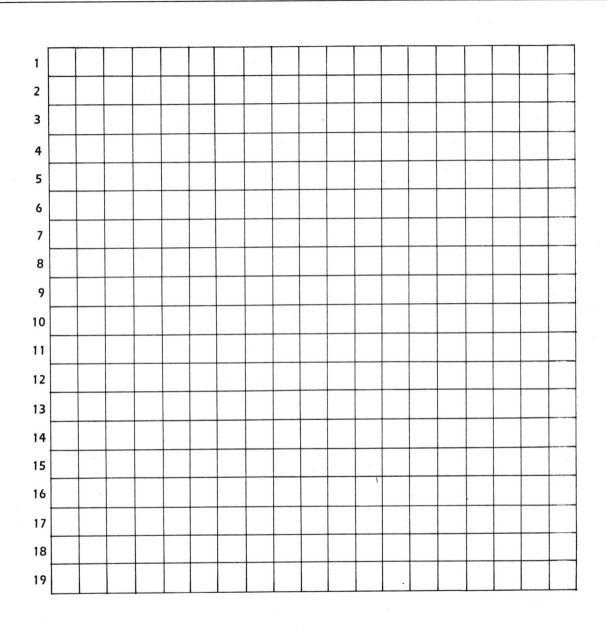

Book list

The following list of books does not represent a fully comprehensive guide to all books suitable for literature-based projects. A lot of books chosen by teachers reflect their own tastes or they will be chosen knowing the likes and dislikes of the children they teach.

However, the following list of books include books which I have tried or those whose titles I have looked at and thought I would like to try in the future.

Picture books

Burglar Bill, Janet and Allan Ahlberg (Armada Picture Lions)
Funny-bones, Janet and Allan Ahlberg (Armada Picture Lions)
Jeremiah in the Dark Woods, Janet and Allan Ahlberg (Armada Picture Lions)
The Moon's Revenge, Joan Aiken (Cape)
The Lighthouse Keeper's Lunch, Ronda and David Armitage (Deutsch/Puffin)
Mr Gumpy's Outing, John Burningham (Cape/Puffin)
Have You Seen My Cat?, Eric Carle (Hodder and Stoughton)
A Mouse's Diary, Michelle Cartlidge (Armada Picture Lions/Heinemann)
Kit and the Magic Kite, Helen Cooper (Hamish Hamilton)
My Friend the Moon, André Dahan (Viking Kestrel)
The Wind Blew, Pat Hutchins (Puffin/Bodley Head)
Mog the Forgetful Cat, Judith Kerr (Armada Picture Lions)
The Cow Who Fell in the Canal, Phyllis Krasilovsky and Peter Spier (Puffin)
The Owl and the Pussycat, Edward Lear (Piccolo)

The Boy Who Held Back the Sea, Thomas Locker (Cape)
The Tiger Who Lost His Stripes, Anthony Paul (Andersen/Beaver)
The Tooth Ball, Philippa Pearce (Deutsch)
Ivor the Engine, Oliver Postgate and Peter Firmin (Armada Picture Lions)
The Rainbow Curtain, Brian Thomas (Hodder and Stoughton)
Joseph and the Amazing Technicolor Dreamcoat, Tim Rice and Andrew Lloyd Webber (Pavilion/Puffin)
I Want My Potty, Tony Ross (Andersen/Armada Picture Lions)
The Fox Went Out on a Chilly Night: an Old Song, Peter Spier (World's Work)
The Selfish Giant, Oscar Wilde (Puffin)

Younger Fiction

Fog Hounds, Wind Cat, Sea Mice, Joan Aiken (Macmillan/Piccolo)
The Railway Cat, Phyllis Arkle (Puffin)
Mouldy's Orphan, Gillian Avery (Puffin)
A Gift From Winklesea, Helen Cresswell (Puffin)
Tales from the 'Wind in the Willows', Kenneth Graham (Puffin)
All about the Giant Alexander, Frank Hermann and George Him (Piccolo)
Bright-eye, Alison Morgan (Puffin)
Grimblegraw and the Wuthering Witch, Barbara Sleigh (Hodder and Stoughton/Puffin)
Gobbolino the Witch's Cat, Ursula Moray Williams (Puffin)

Older Fiction

Watership Down, Richard Adams (Puffin)
Flood Warning, Paul Berna (Puffin)
The TV Kid, Betsy Byars (Bodley Head/Puffin)
Joe and the Gladiator, Catherine Cookson (Puffin)
Over Sea, Under Stone, Susan Cooper (Bodley Head/Puffin)
Moondial, Helen Cresswell (Faber/Puffin)
The Animals of Farthing Wood, Colin Dann (Heinemann/Pan)
Mundo and the Weather-child, Joyce Dunbar (Heinemann/Pan)
The Ghost Downstairs, Leon Garfield (Kestrel/Puffin)
My Side of the Mountain, Jean George (Puffin)
The Giant Under the Snow, John Gordon (Puffin)
Bonny Pit Laddie, Frederick Grice (Puffin)
The Wool-pack, Cynthia Harnett (Puffin)
Which Witch?, Eva Ibbotson (Piccolo)
Stig of the Dump, Clive King (Puffin/Viking Kestrel)
The Jungle Book, Rudyard Kipling (Puffin)
A Wrinkle in Time, Madeleine L'Engle (Puffin)
Wizard of Earthsea, Ursula Leguin (Puffin)
The Magician's Nephew, C S Lewis (Collins/Bodley Head)
The Lion, the Witch and the Wardrobe, C S Lewis (Collins)
The Ghost of Thomas Kempe, Penelope Lively (Heinemann/Puffin)
The Snow Spider, Jenny Nimmo (Magnet/Methuen)
Bedknob and Broomstick, Mary Norton (Dent/Puffin)
Tom's Midnight Garden, Philippa Pearce (OUP/Puffin)
Earthquake, Andrew Salkey (Puffin)
101 Dalmations, Dodie Smith (Piccolo)
Avalanche, A Rutgers Van Der Loeff (Hodder and Stoughton/Puffin)
Charlotte's Web, E B White (Hamish Hamilton/Puffin)
The Little House in the Big Woods, Laura Wilder (Methuen/Puffin)

Children's poetry

A Puffin Book of Verse, compiled by Eleanor Graham (Puffin)
Selected Cautionary Verse, Hilaire Belloc (Puffin)
The Merry Go Round, James Reeves (Puffin)
Old Possum's Book of Practical Cats, T S Eliot (Faber)
The Swinging Rainbow, ed Howard Sergeant (Bell and Hyman)
Figgie Hobbin: Poems for Children, ed Charles Causley (Macmillan/Puffin)
The Young Puffin Book of Verse, compiled by Barbara Ireson (Puffin)
The Puffin Book of Funny Verse, ed Julia Watson (Puffin)
A Single Star, ed David Davis (Puffin)
This Way Delight, Herbert Read (Faber)
Now We Are Six, A A Milne (Methuen)
Oxford Book of Nursery Rhymes, I and P Opie (OUP)
Please Mrs Butler, Allan Ahlberg (Viking Kestrel/Puffin)

Adult poetry

Use adult poetry with older juniors – look at anthologies of poems by the following poets:

- W B Yeats
- Robert Frost
- A E Housman
- John Masefield
- T S Eliot
- Ted Hughes
- John Betjeman

Acknowledgements

The editors and publishers extend their grateful thanks for the reuse of materials first published in *Art and Craft* to: Shiela Freeman for instructions for making a twisted cord in 'Make a Pharaoh' and Alan and Gill Bridgewater for the Egyptian grid system in 'Create a tomb'.

Every effort has been made to trace and acknowledge contributors. If any right has been omitted, the publishers offer their apologies and will rectify this in subsequent editions following notification.

Other Scholastic books

Bright Ideas

The *Bright Ideas* books provide a wealth of resources for busy primary school teachers. There are now more than 20 titles published, providing clearly explained and illustrated ideas on topics ranging from *Writing* and *Maths Activities* to *Assemblies* and *Christmas Art and Craft*. Each book contains material which can be photocopied for use in the classroom.

Teacher Handbooks

The *Teacher Handbooks* give an overview of the latest research in primary education, and show how it can be put into practice in the classroom. Covering all the core areas of the curriculum, the *Teacher Handbooks* are indispensable to the new teacher as a source of information and useful to the experienced teacher as a quick reference guide.

Management Books

The *Management Books* are designed to help teachers to organise their time, classroom and teaching more efficiently. The books deal with topical issues, such as *Parents and Schools* and organising and planning *Project Teaching*, and are written by authors with lots of practical advice and experiences to share.

Let's Investigate

Let's Investigate is an exciting range of photocopiable maths activity books giving open-ended investigative tasks. The series will complement and extend any existing maths programme. Designed to cover the 6 to 12-year-old age range these books are ideal for small group or individual work. Each book presents progressively more difficult concepts and many of the activities can be adapted for use throughout the primary school. Detailed teacher's notes outlining the objectives of each photocopiable sheet and suggesting follow-up activities have been included.